KT-233-626

A Student's Guide to

Things Fall Apart

by
Chinua Achebe

THE LEARNING CENTRE
HAMMERSMITH AND WEST
LONDON COLLEGE
GLIDDON ROAD
LONDON W14 9BL

Paul Callaghan
B.A., M.Ed.

WIZARD

HAMMERSMITH WEST LONDON COLLEGE

328131

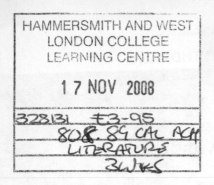

HAMMERSMITH AND WEST
LONDON COLLEGE
LEARNING CENTRE

1 7 NOV 2008

328131   £3-95
808.89 CAL ACH
LITERATURE
3 WKS

Copyright © Wizard Books 2002

All rights reserved.

This book is copyright and protected by Australian and international law. Apart from any fair dealing for the purpose of private study, research or review, as permitted under the Copyright Act, no part may be reproduced by any process or transmitted in any form without written permission. Photocopying more than six pages of this book, even for educational purposes, is against the law and specifically prohibited.

First published in 2002 by
Wizard Books Pty Ltd
ACN 054 644 361
P.O. Box 304 Ballarat 3353 Australia
Email: admin@wizardbooks.com.au
www.wizardbooks.com.au

ISBN 1 876973 21 8

Cover design by Cressaid Media
Cover art by Valerie Den Ouden

Contents

Contents

NOTES ON
THE AUTHOR

Albert Chinualumogu Achebe (pronounced Ar-CHAY-bee) is widely regarded as one of the most important figures in twentieth century African literature. His novel *Things Fall Apart* is world famous, and seen as a landmark work in the study of colonisation.

Achebe was born on November 16, 1930, in Ogidi, Nigeria. His father, Isaiah, had been converted to Christianity and was a teacher in an Anglican missionary school. With his mother, Janet, Isaiah Achebe raised the boy as a Christian. He was also however deeply familiar with traditional ways – his grandparents and extended family having a clear memory of the time before the white man took over. Achebe grew up in a small village, and learn to talk in his people's language, Igbo (Ibo). It was not till the age of eight that he started speaking English as well.

Achebe counts himself fortunate that he was on 'the tail end of that older tradition' (the old village ways). He was told folktales by his mother and older sister, and absorbed the ancient practices of his people. He was deeply interested in the indigenous religion of his people, which was still actively practised in his childhood. Indeed, looking back, and despite his now extensive experience of Western culture, and extended stays in America, he regards village life as having a great many advantages. He has written:

> It was as if [my people] had a choice of creating empires or cities or large communities and they looked at them and said, 'No, we think that what is safest and best is a system in which everybody knows everybody else.' In other words, the village.

This comment is a telling one, in view of what *Things Fall Apart* says about the clash between traditional tribal ways and the imposed new order of the white man.

After elementary and secondary schooling, Achebe attended

Government College, and then University College, Ibadan. Influenced by his studies and emerging national consciousness, he rejected his British name (Albert – after Queen Victoria's husband), taking a shortened form of his indigenous name (Chinua) instead. Then he headed off to England, where he gained a B.A. from London University (1953). He subsequently worked for and studied with the BBC. On his return to Nigeria, he worked in the Nigerian Broadcasting Corporation, as a producer, firstly, then as a program controller (manager).

In 1961, he married Christie Chinwe Okoli, by whom he has had four children: Chinelo (a daughter), Ikkehukwu (a son), Chidi (a son) and Nwando (a daughter). In the same year, he moved into academic life, first as a senior research fellow at the University of Nigeria. By 1973, he was Professor of English at the university. He later visited America, where he was visiting Professor at the University of Massachusetts and the University of Connecticut (1973-76). Later he had periods at the University of California, and posts in Africa. He has been a member of university councils, library boards, arts councils, as well as being deeply involved in publishing (Heinemann, Citadel, and Nigerian publishers).

Achebe's experience straddling the divide between traditional African culture and Western culture awakened him to the conflicts which were at the heart of contemporary Africa. Countries like Nigeria may have gained their independence, but they were still deeply troubled by what had happened to them. The racist contempt of the old colonial authorities was theoretically a thing of the past, but even serious Western writing had offered a largely unsympathetic treatment of tribal Africans. Joseph Conrad had made the continent synonymous with a primitive evil in his famous novella *Heart of Darkness*. Joyce Cary's novel *Mr Johnson* offered the world a comic Nigerian who adores the white man. Achebe found the Conrad work offensively racist and the Cary one 'superficial'. He realised that there was a need to tell the story of how colonisation affected his country 'from the inside'. He was increasingly feeling the urge to express his concerns about his people and country. One critic sums up his preoccupations as three:

> first...the legacy of colonialism at both the individual and societal level; secondly...the fact of English as a language of national and international exchange; thirdly...the obligations and responsibilities

of the writer both to society in which he lives and to his art (G.D.

Killam, *The Novels of Chinua Achebe*, Africana Publishing, 1969) Out of this matrix was to come his output as a writer. When he first set out to write, he deliberately chose English as his medium. Although the language of the colonisers, it is also the language (he knew) that would give him access to the world. He also, naturally, chose to write about his own people, whom he knew so well. Using a traditional narrative form (the life story of a great man), and writing in English, he penned his first novel, *Things Fall Apart*.

The work, published in 1958, made a huge impact, evoking as it does the pain of the post-colonial experience of Africans. Although located clearly in his native Nigeria, the text is effectively a case study of colonisation throughout Africa (and elsewhere too). What struck readers everywhere was the skill with which Achebe takes us inside the mindset of traditional village people, and the force with which he combines what one critic called the 'two main, closely intertwined tragedies [of the novel]: the personal tragedy of Okonkwo...and the public tragedy of the eclipse of one culture by another' (Arthur Ravenscroft, *Chinua Achebe*, Longmans, 1969). The novel was well reviewed (see Critics section), awarded prizes, and brought the 28 year old Achebe to the attention of the world. *Things Fall Apart* was subsequently translated into 50 languages

He went on to produce four more novels, *No Longer at Ease* (1960), *Arrow of God* (1964), *A Man of the People* (1966) and *Anthills of the Savannah* (1988). *Arrow of God* is also about the African experience of colonialism. Set in the 1920s, it concerns the chief priest of an Ibo village who, seeing his traditional power eroded by British colonisation, falls into a tragic decline. The other novels all concern Africa in the era of independence – 'an Africa struggling to regain its footing [after the white invasion] in order to stand on its own two feet'. Critics have praised his fairmindedness and balance.

'His distinction is to have [looked back] without any trace either of chauvinistic idealism or of neurotic rejection, those twin poles of so much African mythologising. Instead, he has recreated for us a way of life which has almost disappeared, and has done so with understanding, with justice and with realism.' (Gerald Moore, *Seven African Writers*, OUP, 1962)

Achebe has also written children's books, poetry, short stories and essays – a total of seventeen books, not to mention innumerable articles and lesser pieces.

Although deeply embedded in the African experience, Achebe's works are also seen as having universal qualities.

Achebe's novels offer a vision of life which is essentially tragic, compounded of success and failure, informed by knowledge and understanding, relieved by humour and tempered by sympathy, embued with an awareness of human suffering and the human capacity to endure.' (Killam, cited above)

NOTES ON

GENRE, STRUCTURE AND STYLE

*T*hings Fall Apart is at heart a 'post-colonial' novel. No matter what else it may do in passing, its primary subject is clearly the transition in Africa from traditional indigenous society to the colonial, white-dominated society imposed by British occupation. The structure of the work could almost be dubbed 'before' (Section 1) and 'after' (Sections 2 and 3) the coming of the white man. While Achebe is in fact careful not to idealise the past, despite a predominantly sympathetic evocation of pre-colonial Africa, readers are left in little doubt about the severe trauma colonisation created. To this extent, like most indigenous and post-colonial texts, *Things Fall Apart* has a clear political message. Implicitly, it challenges the dominance of European culture, and offers a critique of Western values.

Achebe has chosen his material wisely. A diatribe against what the white man did in conquering Africa would most likely fail to engage readers. An account of yet another victim of colonisation might be more emotionally effective, but not rise much above the level of propaganda.

Instead, by giving such a rich and sympathetic account of village life before the coming of the white man, and drawing the reader gently into a position of identification with his indigenous characters, Achebe sets us up to understand the havoc white colonisation played with traditional culture. We don't need to be lectured. The emblematic story of one man's 'fall' says enough. In feeling the tragedy of Okonkwo, we see the human face of what could otherwise have remained just statistics and theory. We feel for indigenous peoples in Africa, and by implication everywhere.

It is probably as well to establish at the outset what we should *not* expect from *Things Fall Apart*. To apply traditional European standards to a text of this kind is inappropriate, for Achebe is writing in a context quite different to what we are familiar with.

In the first instance, this is *not* really a novel of character, though Okonkwo is clearly drawn. The first American edition of the novel was in fact subtitled *The Story of a Strong Man*, but that subtitle has been suppressed in all other editions. As one critic put it:

> *Things Fall Apart* is not a story about character....Achebe could never have called his novel Okonkwo....[The novel], because of its emphasis on community rather than individuality, is a novel of situation rather than of character, and this is undoubtedly its major difference from the traditional Western genre, which...has emphasised the psychological depiction of character. (Charles Larson, *The Emergence of African Fiction*, IUP, 1972)

Okonkwo is important, but he is not the primary subject. He is more an example of the author's subject (the effects of colonisation). What happens to him is important *because* he is representative, or emblematic (of the plight of indigenous Africans as the white man took over their country). He is not a study in personality, like Hamlet – more a study in circumstances, like the principal characters in Holocaust texts (*Night, Elli*, etc).

In the second place, this is not a novel with a complex plot, or highly crafted narrative line. We should not expect the intricacies of a Dickens storyline (eg. *Great Expectations*), let alone those of whodunnit writers. Numerous critics have pointed out that the lengthy first section of the book is almost plotless – a loosely linked series of episodes in the life of Okonkwo's family, without any clear organising structure.

While Sections 2 and 3 are quite different, with a far more dramatic 'fall' story, that means that two thirds of the text are 'formless'. Why? Because the 'documentary' section is intended to draw us inside the culture of Okonkwo, before the 'story' proper begins. Only then can we feel the true pain of what they felt – for we feel it as surrogate insiders. The point of the book is as much identification with the soon-to-be-traumatised Ibo (a recognition of their humanity, their rights, their nobility) – Section 1 – as it is the 'fall' – Sections 2 and 3. The destruction of traditional society caused by white colonisation is easily summarised and can be invoked quickly. A sense of the dignity of traditional society is *not* easily summarised – hence the long, 'plotless', documentary-style exposition.

Thirdly – and this is the hardest of all perhaps to deal with – Achebe does not deliver clear-cut judgements on what is happening, nor divide his characters into 'heroes' and 'villains'. At first, Okonkwo would appear to be the novel's 'hero' – yet he is increasingly a hard man to like. His brutal mistreatment of his wives and children, not to mention the unfortunate Ikemefuna, show him in a less than flattering light. Achebe allows us to see his imperfections all too clearly. The District Commissioner would on the face of it appear to be the novel's 'villain'. But while there is no doubt he's guilty of arrogance and ignorance, he is actually less physically brutal than Okonkwo. Achebe is not exonerating the DC – nor is he excusing him. He is not praising Okonkwo – nor is he dismissing him. He is showing two men caught in a moment of history in which one rose and one fell, and implying that it had as much to do with the vast historical forces acting on both as with the men themselves.

An easy (but dangerous) interpretation of *Things Fall Apart* is that it simply shows the 'good' old order being replaced by the 'bad' new order. It's actually much more complicated than that. Achebe does not just idealise traditional society. We see the violence (Okonkwo is after all a sometime headhunter), the ignorance (remember the throwing away of twins), the disease, the astounding chauvinism (remember Okonkwo advising his sons to be hard on women in order to rule them well). But we also see the happiness, the wisdom, the sense of community, the pride of these traditional people – largely destroyed by the coming of the white man. Traditional stories deliver us a clear moral lesson – who and what is right is plainly identified, and separated from who and what is wrong. Achebe gives us a *mixture* of good and bad, both in the who and the what – leaving it for us to draw what lessons we like from it. It is important, in approaching this novel, to beware of easy conclusions. Things are not as diagrammatic as they seem.

Structurally, as suggested above, the novel is divided into three unequal sections.

SECTION 1 The long 'background' section, detailing traditional life among indigenous Nigerians before white colonisation. It is episodic, moving from one crisis or anecdote in Okonkwo's life to another, without any overriding narrative direction (unless we count the strong impression that Okonkwo is a difficult man who often seems to get into trouble). This is the most lengthy part of the book, taking up 58% of the text.

SECTION 2 This quite brief section (20% of the total) details Okonkwo's 'exile' in his motherland. Like the first section, it is episodic in structure. The difference is that the coming of the white men emerges as a major issue, anticipating the subject matter of the final section.

SECTION 3 This last section, occupying 22% of the text, sees Okonkwo back in his own village. Its principal subject however is not Ibo customs or village anecdotes (as in Section 1), but the relentless intrusions of the white colonists. The last two chapters, in which Okonkwo's 'fall' takes place, move at lightning speed, in stark contrast to the rest of the text. The death of the protagonist is narrated with extraordinarily swiftness, and accompanied by a bewildering shift of perspective (from Okonkwo's, implicitly, though this is not a first person narrative – to that of the District Commissioner). Some readers find this very difficult, and might even consider it a weakness of the text, but as will be argued in the commentary following, the 'lurch' of the novel's ending matches the terrible dislocation of colonisation, as well as making a savage (but unavoidable) point about the way conquerors are the ones who write history.

S tylistically, we need to be aware of subtle things that Achebe is doing, and to avoid Western preconceptions.

For instance, in a text which implicitly celebrates the old ways (though noting their limitations too), we might well expect more 'purple prose' – rhapsodic descriptions of the waterhole at sunset, or the cheery glow of campfires, or *National Geographic* style accounts of the exotic wildlife. Achebe does not provide these delights. Instead, he 'tells tales', very much in the old oral traditional ('I have heard that in some tribes...'). The prose style is plain, without adornments, except for the ever-present Ibo proverbs which are dropped into the conversation of the characters.

Achebe is not setting out to imitate the self-conscious 'literary' cleverness of European writers (the richly theatrical prose of a Dickens, or the polished elegance of a Jane Austen). He is using a type of 'plain man' speech. Look at the opening sentence:

> 'Okonkwo was well known throughout the nine villages and even beyond.'

There is a quiet simplicity about the style, well attuned to the gentle observations of village life which are to follow. There is no hint of high drama. Indeed the first instance of dialogue (direct speech) does not occur till the third page. Most often, the story is told like a tale ('That was many years ago...') being shared around a fireside at night. This is the way the indigenous people told stories, and Achebe mimics their style. Just as their pleasures in their original, unspoiled state were simple ones (food, talk, dancing), so the narrative style of the novel is a simple one.

Several times there are dramatic episodes, and then dialogue features more prominently. We might think of the trial run by the *egwugwu*, or the night journey of Chielo with Ezinma. There are several passages in which elders make long speeches (eg Uchendu's lecture to Okonkwo about suffering in Chapter 14), and here the style becomes quite rich, as befits a type of moral oratory, carrying what are clearly (though indirectly) authorial messages too.

The angle of narration is third person ('Okonkwo was given a plot of ground...'), which allows the author to move between characters at will, describing what Okonkwo is thinking one moment, and Ekwefi's or someone else's perspective another. A first person (I) narrative would have limited Achebe to *one* character's perception. This would have imposed an intolerable burden, given that his main character is an inarticulate man, and the author needs to show differing viewpoints. The wisdom of his choice of narrative angle is most obvious when he makes that famous switch at the end (from Okonkwo to the DC).

Although Achebe is describing what happens from outside the viewpoint of any one individual character, we should note that the 'voice' and consciousness he uses is that of the people themselves (not a modern Westernised African). He does not 'editorialise', or present perspective statements (ie move outside the time and place of the story). For instance, when the white men first appear (Chapter 15), and kill all the people in a village, these events are reported by an Ibo (Obierika), and passed on to the reader without comment. You may recall the term 'iron horse' (bicycle) and the phrase 'used a powerful medicine to make themselves invisible'. Achebe does not translate or comment. He wants us to hear the story from the point of view of the people themselves – not from his or our point of view. He also refuses to offer judgements on what he is depicting. While showing clearly enough the depradations of the colonists, he does not launch into a diatribe against them (as a Dickens would have). He lets the facts, and our accumulated sympathy for his Ibo characters, show the way. Although some readers might have wished for more authorial direction, most critics acknowledge that the discretion of his treatment is one of the strengths of the text.

BACKGROUND NOTES

Nigeria is one of the most populous and economically significant countries in central Africa. It occupies a considerable area of land adjoining the west coast centred on the Niger River (at the gulf half way up the coast). It is a large country, some 1000 km across in both directions (about the size of NSW), with a population of approximately 90,000,000 people. It is rich in oil, tin, rubber and other crops. Its geography ranges from the tropical rainforests of the coastal south through to the semi-arid plains of the north. Its capital is a custom-made city called Abuja (like Canberra) in the centre of the country, though its largest city and major centre is Lagos, on the Atlantic coast.

Human occupation of what we now call Nigeria goes back tens of thousands of years. Most of the people lived in small villages, the largest no more than 2,000 people. These were closely connected by kinship, language (there are three major languages spoken in the country as well as English) and shared traditions. Territory was strongly defended. Tribal wars were commonplace, and the taking of slaves or hostages considered normal. Being predominantly an ancient hunter-gatherer society, Nigerian village life exulted warriors and hunters. Their religions were patriarchal and formidable. Men were privileged in the village communities, although women were accorded a special and honoured (if subservient) role.

Centuries of more or less unchanged life came to an end with the appearance of the Europeans. Northern Nigeria had felt the influence of Islam (around the 13th century), and southern people had limited contact with Portuguese traders in the 15th. Then came the slave trade – from roughly the 1480 through to the mid 1800s. The Gulf of Benin was a major stopping place for slave ships. Vast numbers of captured

Africans were taken to Benin and Lagos for loading onto ships bound for the new American colonies. The locals themselves helped the Europeans. They thought entirely in tribal terms, and were perfectly happy to sell people from other tribes captured in war to the white man. In time, a significant proportion of the estimated 30,000,000 African slaves exported to the Americas went through Nigeria.

Then, in the nineteenth century, the major European countries found a new way of exploiting Africa. When they realised that it was rich in timber, gold, oil, gum and minerals, they quite simply invaded it and divided it up between them. In 1861, ostensibly to stem the slave trade (for slavery had been outlawed in England), the British occupied Lagos, and made the country a major part of its trade. British missionaries journeyed to what was then portrayed as 'darkest Africa' (dark in the double sense of dark-skinned, and heathen, or evil), and set up schools and Christian communities. Needless to say, conversion (to Christianity) was a condition of entry to church-run schools (the only ones). In 1884, Great Britain claimed the whole country as its colony, although it took till 1903 for the entire population to come under strict control. In 1914, Nigeria was declared a British 'Protectorate' (read colony in all but name). British companies had free access to Nigerian resources and the white man lived a life of privilege.

While British authority may have brought relative stability for a time, and introduced some useful western inventions (such as literacy and a legal system), it also wrought untold damage to the indigenous people. For a start, the nation of 'Nigeria' was a British fiction. The very name was the invention of an English journalist. Geographically, it was not one nation but three – the Moslem Fulani of the north, the Yoruba of the southwest and (after colonisation) the largely Christian Ibo of the southeast. The population of this new conglomerate nation were divided by language, custom and religion. The already well developed ethnic divisions got worse under the British, who favoured the Christianised Ibo, promoting them to administrative positions over other ethnic groups. This would eventually lead to the appalling Civil War (Biafran War) of 1967-70, which saw large numbers of Ibo slaughtered by their vengeful compatriots. The more rebellious north was seriously under-resourced in colonial times, creating a lasting bitterness and division. British missionaries caused enormous change to the local culture, and together with the superior attitudes of the administration, left Nigerians feeling inferior culturally, economically and socially. The scars left by British occupation are still felt in modern Nigeria.

After the Second World War, a modified form of independence was set up, though with British assistance. In 1963, Nigeria became a completely free Republic. However, despite great natural advantages, the country has continued to suffer in the post-colonial era. It has endured a series of coups, short-term governments, assassinations, corruption trials, and in the shocking 'Biafran War' (when the Ibo minority declared its independence from the rest of the country and held out for nearly three years until forced to surrender), mass murder. It is worth noting that Achebe's later novels deal extensively with the post-colonial legacy in his native country, one which has been deeply troubled (as explained briefly above).

Since *Things Fall Apart* deals with a society so different from our own, and since cultural prejudice is an ever-present danger, a few notes on Nigerian culture might be in order.

In middle class, city dwelling Nigeria today, there are strong similarities with western lifestyle. Out in the country, however, things are largely unchanged. Marriage customs are highly complex, and involve what (to western eyes) seem like extremely chauvinistic elements. For instance, a woman taken in marriage still has a 'bride price', or dowry (to use the European term), which may be crops, animals, or a promise of labour on the father's farm. In traditional African terms however this is not insulting, but a legitimate form of transaction, and the source of much pride. Particularly in the Moslem parts of the country, a man who is wealthy enough may take several wives. Like the bride price, this is partly an interface between social and economical necessities, partly religious, partly an offshout of the patriarchal mindset of the culture. Polygamy is not considered sinful, but sensible. The wives work together co-operatively, share the child-minding and emotional burdens and take turns preparing food for the husband, who sleeps in his own hut, so as not to be seen as having a favourite (and therefore destabilising the relationship of the wives). If a husband dies, she/they may go (together with his property) to his brother, for care and protection.

Religious beliefs vary enormously in Nigeria. The Ibo (source material for the novel) were traditionally polytheistic (many gods), before Christianity, and believed in the existence of spirits. They were particularly concerned with bad spirits, who were thought to haunt the living, and had to be appeased by sacrifice or by digging up and burning the bones of the ancestor believed to be the source of the spirit. In religious festivals, important men of the village dress up in elaborate masks and costumes, impersonating the spirit of a god or ancestor. Like people everywhere, the Nigerians believe in a set of 'rules' for living, and believe that bad behaviour has dangerous spiritual (and physical) consequences.

A major part of what Achebe is doing in his novel is sympathetically evoking a traditional tribal culture. It is vital to remember that the proper way to approach the story is with an open mind, accepting the traditional ways the author portrays for what they are – part of a balanced, fulfilling social fabric that was handed down for centuries – and not as cause for derision or premature criticism (in the light of modern and entirely alien social perspectives).

SUMMARY AND COMMENTARY

PART ONE

Chapter 1

We are introduced to Okonkwo (pronounced O-KON-kwo), the principal character of the story. Okonkwo is regarded as a great man in the village. Ever since he beat a famous wrestler (Amalinze the Cat) as a young man, he has been regarded as a significant person.

His father, Unoka, had been quite different. He was a 'failure' – poor, cowardly and unreliable. He constantly borrowed money, and never paid it back. On one occasion, a man to whom he owed money came to visit him. When Unoka realised that his friend was asking ever so politely for a repayment, Unoka sent him on his way laughing. In consequence, Okonkwo, who was ashamed of his father, made it his business to become a success.

This opening chapter introduces us to the protagonist, Okonkwo. We might note the description of him as a tall, 'severe' man, quick to anger and impatient with others. Achebe motivates him quite clearly. The account of Unoka explains why Okonkwo's desire to be 'strong' was so compelling. His shame at his father's irresponsible ways have obviously caused overcompensation. Thus the young man has grown up determined to be tough and successful, to gain honour where his father had none.

However, while we know very little of Okonkwo at this stage, and indeed the indications are predominantly positive, we might note the subtle hints about the dangers of such a personality. 'He had no patience with unsuccessful men', we read. He walked 'as if he was going to pounce on somebody'. We might note that he compensates for his slight stammer (clearly a result of inferiority and nervousness) by becoming angry. Though subtle indications, these are nonetheless the signs of a driven personality with the potential for aggression. Indeed the very pride which has already been foregrounded in the character itself, has the potential to be a danger. We might even perhaps be reminded of the traditional warnings (in literature and religion) accorded the 'sin' of pride. In flight from his father's incompetence, Okonkwo seems to have become not just 'one of the greatest men of his time', but one of the *proudest*. In this, is there the seed of some fall (as implied by the title of the novel)?

Chapter 2

Okonkwo is woken one night by the sound of the town crier, calling a meeting the following day. In the morning, all the men of the tribe meet in the market place. The tribal orator informs them that a daughter of Umuofia (the name of the town) has been murdered by the men of a neighbouring town, Mbaino. Okonkwo, being an important man, is despatched to Mbaino to demand reparation. He returns to Umuofia with the virgin and young boy demanded as a means of averting war. The young girl is given as a new wife to the bereaved man. The boy, Ikemefuna, is taken temporarily into Okonkwo's household, and given to Okonkwo's most senior wife to be looked after.

We are informed about the 'heavy' hand with which Okonkwo rules his three wives and eight children. We also learn about the layout of Okonkwo's compound.

Let us note two things about this chapter. First there is the matter of the war averted with Mbaino. While our initial reaction may be to be horrified by the raw passion of the tribal meeting, and indeed by the 'barbaric' compensation (a virgin and a boy), we should not overlook the suggestion, well and truly built into the text, that the tribe is in fact behaving justly and reasonably. Rather than engaging precipitously in bloodshed, they are demanding reparation, very much as we would expect in our own civil courts. The fact that the compensation payment takes human form is startling, but hardly surprising, for what is obviously a traditional tribal society. In a context where women are routinely given as wives to men, a virgin is the obvious compensation from a man whose wife has been killed.

The young boy, clearly to be the subject of more of the story, is a type of hostage. Thus, what might be an initial reaction of horror, turns on reflection, into one of cautiously appreciating the sanity of what has just happened.

The other thing clearly to emerge from this chapter is further information about the 'demons' motivating Okonkwo. We read that 'his whole life was dominated by fear, the fear of failure and weakness...the fear of himself'. Like many a person in any culture, Okonkwo has found a way of coping with his imagined weakness by converting it into the opposite of what he fears. That this hint has now been played out in consecutive chapters attests to the significance it has in the psychological scheme of the novel. Here is a man forcing himself to be something other than what he would naturally wish to be. Therein lies the danger. We note also his 'heavy hand' with his wives and oldest son, who is already a 'sad-faced youth' as a result of his father's harassment. The effects of Okonkwo's obsession are only too plain. His 'greatness' and prosperity are thus shown to be belied by a nagging inner insecurity, and the seed of what may be his greatest weakness (his aggression and impetuosity).

Chapter 3

We are given an account of the difficult start in life that Okonkwo had. His old father Unoka had once gone to the Oracle to find out if he had offended the gods (on account of his poor harvests). The priestess of the god angrily told him to go away and 'work like a man'. Okonkwo, realising that he had to start from scratch, went to a wealthy man in his village, Nwakibie, presenting him with gifts, and humbly asking to borrow yams. Impressed by Okonkwo's diligence and politeness, Nwakibie gave him yams. Unfortunately, that season saw first a dreadful drought, followed by unexpected rain. It was only with difficulty that Okonkwo survived the year. However, his endless work and survival confirmed him in his 'inflexible will'. He was by then supporting his mother, father and sisters almost on his own.

Traditionally, a tragedy concerns a great man brought low. Far more than the opening story of Okonkwo's defeating the wrestler called the Cat, this story of the yams is, in the terms of the native culture which is the story's context, a testimony to Okonkwo's greatness. Not only has he broken with the laziness of his father, not only has he humbly gone to the man in his village, not only has he diligently worked to produce his own first crops, but he has endured the twin disasters of drought and flood. All this is testimony to Okonkwo's strength of character. Once again however we note the subtle references to a 'proud heart' (to pride). What makes Okonkwo a great man, in the moral and psychological scheme of the novel, also makes him a vulnerable man.

Chapter 4

Okonkwo insults a man with no titles at a village meeting, calling him a woman. One of the old men reproves him, and he apologises. Later however he commits an even greater sin, beating his youngest wife Ojiugo during the Week of Peace, when she fails to cook his evening meal in time. The priest of the earth goddess comes to Okonkwo and despite his attempts at explanation, ordains a punishment for Okonkwo.

Meanwhile Ikemefuna has begun to recover from his initial terror at being forced to live with Okonkwo's family. He becomes a favourite in the family, and is even liked by Okonkwo – though Okonkwo will never show any such emotion openly. Indeed, during the days of yam preparation, he treats both Nwoye, his son, and Ikemefuna roughly, thinking he is preparing them for the difficult job of manhood.

This chapter offers us two more episodes in the continuing saga of Okonkwo's history of pride. We are reminded of how lacking in understanding Okonkwo is. There is the insult he levels at the untitled man during the village meeting. There is also, more seriously, the beating of his wife Ojiugo during the Week of Peace. In both instances, by the way, we are reminded of the profound and essential wisdom of the tribal culture. In the first instance, it is a wiser old man who reminds Okonkwo of his moral duty: 'Those whose palm kernels were cracked for them by a benevolent spirit should not forget to be humble'. In the second case it is the priest of the goddess, who reminds Okonkwo that 'We live in peace with our fellows to honour our great goddess of the earth without whose blessing our crops will not grow. You have committed a great evil'. The great evil is of course not just the breaking of the goddess' sacred law – it is the far more universal moral law of the need to live in peace with other people.

Chapter 5

The Feast of the New Yam arrives. Great preparations precede it, as well as a feeling of excitement. Okonkwo however is restless – he finds festivals and socialising not to his taste. His irritability breaks out when he finds what he believes is a banana tree that has been killed. His second wife Ekwefi admits to taking branches. Okonkwo beats her. When she adds insult to injury by making a disparaging remark, he takes the gun with which he is about to go hunting and shoots at her. She is not hurt.

The second day of the festival is devoted to wrestling. Ekwefi is a very keen fan – years before she fell in love with Okonkwo after he beat The Cat at a wrestling competition, and left her husband for Okonkwo. The wives prepare food for the festival. The daughters bring the food prepared by the wives to Okonkwo, sitting in his hut.

Chapter 5 continues to background for us the culture of these indigenous people. The sacred festival of the yams is described in sympathetic detail, as are the various preparations made for the festival. We find ourselves reading descriptions of the polygamous marriage of Okonkwo – our doubtless reluctance about the arrangement shading into understanding of how in practice such a situation worked. The cooperation between the various wives and children is clear. Achebe is obviously describing a situation very different from what we are used to, but doing so sympathetically – putting us *inside* an alien culture in a way which is most instructive and aids our understanding of these people.

One point needs special mention: the outburst of anger which leads to Okonkwo beating Ekwefi. Naturally, our reaction is one of horror, particularly when Okonkwo follows this up with the ill-conceived gunshot which could have left Ekwefi dead or seriously injured. Again we are reminded of the impetuous, not to say dangerously aggressive, aspects of Okonkwo's nature. These are being signposted very clearly for us – and need to be borne in mind as we see how Okonkwo deals with the later challenges of the white man.

Chapter 6

The wrestling begins – to the great pleasure of all the villagers. Ekwefi talks to Chielo – in ordinary life a widow who is a good friend and very fond of Ekwefi's only daughter, Ezinma. When possessed by the spirit, Chielo becomes the priestess of Agbala, the Oracle of Hills and the Caves. The wrestling continues, with older and more experienced fighters. Finally the leaders of the two teams battle one another until one is victorious. The crowd is exultant.

Achebe describes the wrestling in rich detail – enabling us to readily make a connection between our own experience of the excitement of watching sport, and the similar experience of these Nigerian people of more than a century ago. Once again it is the connection we are able to make between our own experience and theirs which is an important part of what the author is doing. We might note in passing that the celebration of physical prowess – typical of a warrior culture such as this – is uppermost. The last line of the chapter – 'then send him word to fight for us' (referring to the triumphant wrestler) – reminds us of the cultural context. This is a society in which the ability to fight and defend territory and kin is extremely important. We should remember this if our initial reaction is squeamishness about the 'warrior' aspects of this society.

Chapter 7

Okonkwo likes to have Nwoye, his son, and Ikemefuna, his adopted son (the hostage from the neighbouring tribe), with him, as he tells them 'masculine stories of violence and bloodshed' – to toughen them and prepare them for life as a man. Nwoye however prefers the gentler animal folk tales told by his mother.

One day, a locust plague descends on the village – to the great joy of the people – for locusts make good eating. Okonkwo's eating of the locusts however is interrupted by an elder of the village, who tells him that the Oracle has pronounced the death sentence on Ikemefuna. The man instructs Okonkwo not to 'bear a hand in his death', for the boy calls him father. The following day, Ikemefuna is given the story that he is to be taken home. Surrounded by the men of the village, he goes off into the forest, full of trepidation. Finally, one of the men raises his matchet (machete) to kill the boy. Okonkwo, hearing the boy's cry, finishes the job – since he is 'afraid of being thought weak'.

News of the death of his friend causes Nwoye to feel a terrible pain in his heart.

More so even than the beating of Ekwefi or the rough treatment of his sons by Okonkwo, the murder of Ikemefuna tests our sympathy for and patience with the traditional practices of these people. Achebe is deliberately showing us *both* sides of the old ways. We have plentiful examples already of the benign aspects of the traditional Ibo village culture. We now have a stark reminder of the brutal sides of that culture. In a hunter/gatherer society dominated by war and the need for warrior qualities, the taking of slaves or hostages, and the arbitrary killing of anyone deemed an 'enemy' is routine (and indeed understandable).

The death of the boy, an innocent victim of this harsh law and the evidently arbitrary whim of the Oracle, is a reminder that we should *not* unthinkingly glamorise traditional ways. One of the tendencies of post colonial and anti-colonial writers is to idealise what went before – portraying traditional ways as wondrous, and new (Europeanised) ways as a degradation. It is not as simple as this, as the death of Ikemefuna makes clear. We feel for Nwoye when he senses something 'give way inside him'. Achebe makes a link between his horrified reaction at the death of his friend and his horror at once hearing abandoned babies in the forest cry (the traditional culture saw twins as an evil sign – to be put away). Let us not therefore overly romanticise Ibo culture. It is not that simple.

Chapter 8

For two days after the death of Ikemefuna, Okonkwo cannot eat. He drinks heavily and is unable to sleep. Finally his wives put food in front of him and Ezinma urges him to eat. Okonkwo berates himself for behaving like an old woman.

To distract himself, he goes to see his friend Obierika. Obierika tells him that a suitor is coming together with his relatives to discuss the bride price for Obierika's daughter. He invites Okonkwo to participate. Okonkwo tells him he should have come on the outing which saw the death of Ikemefuna, but Obierika replies that he was not asked to go. He adds that Okonkwo should not have done the deed himself because it 'would not please the Earth'. He is told about the death of an old man of the village, whose oldest wife died immediately after the husband.

Okonkwo goes to share in the setting of the bride price for Obierika's daughter. The girl is brought in before the men and approved of. After sharing wine, they engage in a setting of the bride price. Later, when all is decided, they discuss the strange habits of other villages and tribes, who do the same thing in oddly different ways. The subject moves to other cultures, including even the white man.

Okonkwo's reaction to the death of his adopted son is a very interesting one. It is perfectly clear that the boy's death is extremely distressing to Okonkwo – the drinking and the refusal to eat a clear sign of the trauma. Yet he cannot reconcile his misery over what he has done with his view of himself as a tough man. 'Okonkwo, you have become a woman indeed', he says in perplexity, when he realises how deeply the incident has affected him. Tragedy is too strong a word for what is going on here (except for what happened to the boy). We do however see a deep-seated conflict between Okonkwo's vision of what he should be as a man and his genuine feelings of affection for the boy. Once again we are aware of Okonkwo's personality problems – the potentially fatal conflict between what his finer feelings tell him to do and what his sense of personal dignity and manhood urge him towards.

The bride price ceremony is an interesting example of Achebe's account of pre-colonial life in Africa. It is another instance of how a reader's initially reluctant attitude – along the lines of 'How they could possible sell a woman as a wife?' – gradually shades into a sense of how well-managed the transaction was. Achebe does not editorialise or lecture – he does not argue that the traditional way of doing things is the proper way and that modern ways are inappropriate – he simply shows that the old practices were done with style and some sensitivity.

As a matter of curiosity the white men are mentioned for the first time at the end of this chapter – though at this stage they are merely a passing reference (probably to some missionary glimpsed by a person journeying to another part of the country), and not an active force in the life of these people. That is to come later.

Chapter 9

Okonkwo is woken one morning by Ekwefi, who is in dread that her daughter Ezinma is dying. Although others say that it is only *iba* (the fever), Ekwefi is terrified that it is the evil spirit. We are told that Ekwefi has borne ten children – nine of whom died in infancy, leaving only Ezinma. There is a belief in the village that Ezinma is one of the *Ogbanje*, a mischievous spirit who is reborn in children. Although only the year before the medicine man had been called and had found the special *iyi-uwa*, a talisman identifying the *Ogbanje*, now Ezinma is sick again. Okonkwo goes to the forest and brings back medicinal plants, orders them boiled, and then insists that Ezinma breathes the vapours. Later she is sent to bed.

The events of this chapter (on the face of it) might horrify us. Although it is never acknowledged explicitly by the author, the unscientific principles involved in the diagnosis of illness and disease are (implicitly) a serious problem for these people. Unexplained infant mortality – no doubt really attributable to insanitary conditions or the spreading of disease through bacteria or viral infection – is beyond their comprehension. They see instead the operation of evil spirits. Yet it is *not* appropriate to laugh (at the spirits idea), or to see this as some sort of indirect justification of colonisation. It is merely an honest acknowledgement of how things were in a pre-scientific culture. And we should note what Okonkwo's remedy says about traditional knowledge of herbal remedies. The notion of bacteria and the spread of disease by microscopic organisms may be unknown to these people, who did not have the benefit of a scientific tradition, but the healing properties of naturally occurring substances *is* known. We should not write them off as 'ignorant' – merely as lacking in certain types of knowledge.

      The other aspect to note in this chapter is the powerful feeling of Ekwefi for her surviving child. When we read that Ekwefi had difficulty 'bonding' with Ezinma, and suffered so much from the apprehension that her only child would die, we see in her qualities which any parent feels for any child in danger. The despair ('she believed because it was that faith alone that gave her own life any kind of meaning') is palpable, and we feel very strongly indeed for her. By this means again, Achebe bridges the gap of time and culture between us and these people.

Chapter 10

All the people of Umuofia gather for a 'trial'. The village elders, dressed in the masks and costumes of *egwugwu* (ancestral spirits) come out ceremonially into the square. After ritual address, the sides of the case present their stories. Uzowulu claims that his in-laws should pay him back the bride price for his wife, who has returned to her people. Then they hear the other side. The oldest brother of the woman claims that her husband has beaten her savagely and *that* is the reason she has left him. The *egwugwu* withdraw and consult with one another. Then they make the pronouncement. They order Uzowulu to take a pot of wine to his in-laws and beg his wife to return. The ancestral spirit adds 'it is not bravery when a man fights with a woman'. They also instruct the brother to allow the wife to return to her husband when this ceremonial duty has been observed. The trial ends.

We must not allow ourselves to be distracted by the magical theatrics of the occasion – the masks and costumes, the smoke and the ritual phrases. These clearly are part of the traditional belief system of the people and meant to enhance the dignity of the occasion (not unlike judges' wigs and robes or the special costumes worn by professionals such as medical people). What is really important is the justice (or otherwise) of the proceedings. And here we must concede that a great deal of wisdom is shown. The traditional communal justice system – allowing both sides of the case to be heard by the *egwugwu* – is exactly equivalent, for all its supernatural paraphernalia, to a civil trial in our own western society. Both sides are heard, and a wise judgement – in effect a negotiated settlement – is arranged. Because the decision is perceived to be lawful by the community itself (represented by its ancestral spirits) the decision is accepted and the combatants cease their bitter standoff. It is difficult not to applaud such a wise resolution. If the effect of the previous chapter was to suggest that the Ibo were 'primitive' and vulnerable, the effect of this chapter is to show that in the terms of justice traditional ways were profoundly wise.

Chapter 11

It is a very dark night. The children are in their various huts listening to stories told by their mothers. Ekwefi tells Ezinma the story of tortoise – a folk tale about how the tortoise came to have multiple parts of his shell which do not fit together neatly. Just as Ezinma is beginning to tell a story of her own, they will hear the voice of Chielo, the priestess of Agbala. Chielo is possessed with the goddess. Loudly she calls for Ezinma. Brushing aside Okonkwo's pleadings and the evasions of Ekwefi, she insists on taking the child with her. While Ekwefi watches horrified, the priestess takes the child on her back and sets off into the dark night.

Ekwefi, unable to resist, follows the priestess for a long time. Eventually Chielo and the girl disappear into the entrance of the cave of the goddess. Ekwefi is startled when she sees a figure. It is Okonkwo, who has been following them both. They wait outside the cave of the goddess until dawn. Ekwefi remembers back to the night she left her husband and first gave herself to Okonkwo.

The first part of this chapter is devoted largely to the retelling of the folk tale. While it is easy enough to interpret this as yet another example of the rich cultural 'documentary' information provided by the author, a closer reading suggests other qualities that we might note in the folk tale. Among these are the wit – most obvious in the name tortoise chooses for himself ('All of you'), the beautiful structure of the tale, which moves quickly from the exposition to the climax, and the revenge pay off, and the way the tale matches aspects of the subject matter (such as the fat profile of a tortoise – commensurate with the character in the story of a glutton who stuffs himself with food and drink).

The second part of the chapter is devoted of course to the seizing of Ezinma by Chielo, the priestess. We already know that Chielo is a close friend (in ordinary life) of Ekwefi, and particularly fond of Ezinma. What we may deduce, reading between the lines, is that Chielo, after the dangerous episode of *iba*, is concerned to bring the child under the influence of the goddess. In the character of the priestess, 'possessed', Chielo takes the girl to the sacred place, presumably for blessing or spiritual protection. The fact that the whole episode is cloaked in magical elements should not distract us overly from the obviously benign intentions of the woman. The other thing that emerges is the concern of Okonkwo. Although he is unable to express it in words, and indeed veils his concern with mockery, we can actually see that he has taken more than a normal interest in the whole episode. He has come after his wife and child out of a deep concern for them. The last paragraph of the chapter, which reminds readers that the marriage was one of love and not of convenience, offers another (and much more sympathetic) way of looking at the couple.

Chapter 12

We are told what happened afterwards. At dawn, Chielo came out of the cave, and without even acknowledging Okonkwo and Ekwefi, returned Ezinma to her bed.

That day is the *uri* (betrothal) of Obierika's son to his wife-to-be. All the village is involved in the extensive preparations for the celebration. Although there is a brief episode when a cow escapes and has to be rounded up, the preparations go well. The in-laws arrive, and the ceremony proceeds, with drinking, mutual praise of the in-laws, admiring of the beautiful bride, and much dancing.

Once again the texture of life in these times is richly rendered. The joyful communal participation – for all the village rejoice in the marriage – is made perfectly clear. While the ceremony and its participants are very different from a western style marriage, we might note that the bride is treated with great respect and indeed the whole ceremony is a masterly example of collaboration. Like other scenes in the book thus far, the betrothal ceremony leaves us with a strong sense of how fulfilling life was in those times.

Chapter 13

The village is awakened to the news of the death of one of the clan. It is the old man Ezeudu (who warned Okonkwo about not taking a hand in the killing of Ikemefuna). Because he was a great man in the clan, the funeral celebrations are massive, with the participation of *egwugwu* and all the people of the village. Great speeches are made to celebrate the life of the dead man.

Right in the midst of the funeral celebrations a horrible discovery is made – the dead man's son lies in a pool of blood. Okonkwo gun has exploded, inadvertently killing the boy. Okonkwo must now flee the clan, for he has committed a crime against the Earth goddess. His friends help move some of his belongings. Then, under cover of darkness, Okonkwo and his wives and children leave the village. As dawn breaks, the men of the village demolish Okonkwo's compound utterly. Obierika, his friend, reflects sadly on the way such calamities take place.

To the list of rituals in the old order which we have witnessed must now be added of that of a funeral. As with the betrothal, the trial and other ceremonies, so too we see in the funeral of the great man the wisdom and cultural richness of the Ibo people. The eulogy is eloquent. The grief of the community at the passing of this great man is genuine. The communal spirit is clearly involved. The rich and complex customs of these people is very sympathetically evoked.

However, once again, Okonkwo is seen to have fatal qualities. Although the explosion which causes the death of the boy is entirely an accident, we cannot help associating it in our mind with Okonkwo's warrior qualities. Is this some sort of curse? Earlier, he had committed the sin of killing his surrogate son (Ikemefuna), despite the specific warning of this very man, whose own son he has now inadvertently killed. If there is a curse involved, is it because Okonkwo is hasty, warlike, aggressive? Certainly the text submits to such an interpretation.

PART TWO

Chapter 14

Okonkwo and his family are received by his mother's people in their village. The head of the family is his mother's surviving brother, Uchendu. Okonkwo is given land on which to plant his yams (contributed by his kinsmen), as well as help to build a compound and huts for himself and his wives and children. After the long summer drought, the rain comes at last, to everyone's relief. Okonkwo works hard, but his heart is not in it. His great ambition – 'to become one of the lords of the clan' – is no more.

One day, Uchendu calls all his family together – as well as Okonkwo. He asks them all why one of the most common names the clan give to their children is Nneka – 'Mother is Supreme'. No one knows the answer. Uchendu then tells them all that although the men rule and the father is the head of the family, it is to the mother that children go for comfort. He tells Okonkwo that he has come to his motherland in his time of need, and that he should not insult his mother's spirit by despairing. If he does so, says Uchendu, they may all die in exile. He reminds Okonkwo that he is not the greatest sufferer in the world – giving examples of his own bereavements and that of his family.

Like all major literary texts, *Things Fall Apart* offers up insights which go well beyond the local issues of its particular time and place. Achebe is at pains in his novel to draw us into the lives of his Nigerian villagers, to feel for them as their time of crisis approaches. He is also keen to show the universality of human experience (and indeed that is a large part of why we empathise so readily with his characters). In this chapter, the universality of suffering is the issue addressed. Some critics have pointed out that it is a recurrent theme in the author's work. Be that as it may, Achebe's treatment of the theme here is highly significant. It doesn't matter that the speaker is an illiterate tribal elder in Nigeria and the time well over a century ago. Some things don't change, and our experience of misfortune is one of them.

What does Achebe draw us to contemplate? Okonkwo, his ambitions thwarted, his pride severely damaged, has fallen into despair ('everything had been broken'). He sees himself as 'the greatest sufferer in the world' (as Uchendu bluntly puts it), and the future as hopeless. Now it is this perception, or delusion (we might venture to call it) which the wise old man Uchendu addresses in his lengthy and noble speech. Uchendu first reminds him of his responsibility: 'if you allow sorrow to weigh you down and kill you, they [his wives and children] will all die in exile'. This is the other side of Okonkwo's enjoyment of leadership (he cannot insist on being the boss and then give up when things turn uncomfortable). We are not told by the author, but can deduce that such an argument (to Okonkwo's pride) will bear fruit. Uchendu then reminds Okonkwo that many others have problems far greater than Okonkwo's (banishment for life, the death of children or wives), and that he must make an effort to get beyond the misery and find the strength to go on.

If we think about modern psychotherapy, we would have to conclude that it often centres on exactly these issues. Someone has an unhappy childhood, or suffers from a setback or even tragedy. Life (as Uchendu reminds us in the final lines of the chapter) is full of such possibilities. What then? Despair and death – or grieving, followed by coping and survival? Face your responsibilities, says Uchendu; remember that all people suffer, and someone will always have problems greater than your own. The old man is wise, and the message is a universal one.

Chapter 15

Two years have passed. One day, Okonkwo is visited by his old friend, Obierika. Uchendu welcomes him and they exchange news. One of the shocking pieces of news is that the village, Abame has been wiped out. Obierika tells the story. Three months ago, a white man appeared in the village. He was riding an 'iron horse' (a bicycle). The villagers consulted their Oracle, who prophesied 'that the strange man would break their clan and spread destruction among them'. The Oracle also foretold that other white men were coming, 'like locusts'. The villagers killed the white man. Time passed, and other white men came. One day, when the village was full for the market, the white men used a 'powerful medicine' and killed everyone in the village.

Uchendu is convinced that they were foolish, because they killed a man who said nothing (they could not of course understand a word he said). Okonkwo is convinced they were foolish because they did not arm themselves. He thought the stories about white men were made up.

Obierika explains that he has brought Okonkwo the cowrie shells (money) for Okonkwo's yams back in his home village. Okonkwo thanks him profusely.

This chapter sees the first definitive appearance of white colonists (though this expression is not used). We note that the first encounter is, ominously, a fatal one. On the face of it, the destruction of Abame is just a tragedy of misunderstanding (the villagers seeing the white missionary as an evil spirit and killing him – the white authorities seeing the villagers as murderous savages, and killing them in reprisal). At a deeper or perhaps one could say symbolic level, in fact, the Oracle is right – the strangers would indeed, in the fullness of time, 'break their clan and spread destruction'. Only the role of the first man was overstated. It would not be him, but his compatriots, the rest of the European 'locusts' (an apt metaphor, when we remember how these creatures take over and feed off a land), who would effect the destruction. We realise that though the events described are at a remove from the central characters, they are a harbinger of the doom that is about to befall them.

We cannot leave this chapter without considering the 'post mortems' (or analysis) of Uchendu and Okonkwo. Uchendu uses traditional wisdom to interpret what happened. He believes the tragedy happened because the villagers ignored the bad magic of killing a man who says nothing. The folk tale about Mother Kite is a way of saying that destroying what you don't understand is dangerous. There is an obvious seed of truth in this. It could be argued that it was the hasty reaction of the Abame villagers (killing what they didn't understand) which brought about their destruction. However, the quaint logic of folk tales was never going to hold off such a thing as the onslaught of Westernisation in Africa, and really, magic had little to do with it. So it is with Okonkwo's judgement. For him, everything comes down the way of the warrior. In his analysis, the villagers were weak because they did not arm themselves to fight back. Again there is a superficial truth in this, in the short term, but no comfort in the long term (the white attackers would have simply come back with more soldiers at another time). Neither magic nor war were ever going to prevent the white man from taking Africa. Achebe does not tell us this. But as we think about the text, we might draw this melancholy conclusion from what he depicts.

Chapter 16

Two years later, Obierika pays another visit to his friend. This time the reason is that he has been startled to find Nwoye (Okonkwo's son) amongst the missionaries who have come to Umuofia. Okonkwo does not wish to talk about it, but Obierika hears the story anyway.

The white men had visited Mbanta (the village in which Okonkwo lives in exile). One white man and a number of Ibo converts arrived. They told the villagers that they had come to live among the people, bringing their iron horses (bicycles) and their god. The missionary told the people that their god was the only true god, and that the people's gods were useless. The villagers thought the missionary and his converts crazy. However, when they all burst into song, the Ibo people were entranced. Okonkwo left after a while, disgusted with the newcomers. However Nwoye was 'captivated'. Something in the new religion touched the yearning in his heart and the unanswered questions he had had about the indigenous faith.

The thin end of the colonialising wedge was religion. Presenting themselves in peace, so that the indigenous people treated them as unthreatening curiosities (not as a warlike invasion force), the missionaries insinuated themselves stealthily into the culture of the Ibo. With their mysterious 'iron horses' and beguiling songs (hymns), they were perceived as a harmless novelty, and allowed to stay. But their influence soon began to be felt. They also presented an alternative to the rigours of indigenous culture. We read that Nwoye saw 'the poetry of the new religion', which answered his long suppressed dread of the warrior aspects of his father's character, and his horror of the harsher things in his own culture (abandoning twins, the decree which led to the death of Ikemefuna).

Achebe is acknowledging that the coming of the white man was *not* entirely a one-way, 100% bad intrusion (though that is commonly presented as the truth by anti-colonial writers). Christianity, we assume, offered legitimate benefits to some people. Of course it did not suit tough old fighters like Okonkwo, but it *did* speak to gentler souls, like Nwoye. We know enough about the dynamics of the father-son relationship here to see that something that gave Nwoye a chance at a new identity, or rekindled self-esteem (as a Christian), had a lot of appeal.

Chapter 17

The missionaries had asked the village elders for a place to build their church. Thinking themselves very clever, the elders had given them the 'evil forest' (the place where bad spirits and the rejected dead were buried). Gleefully, the villagers awaited the inevitable wrath of the gods. However, nothing happened: the missionaries were totally unharmed.

The village people began to be converted to the new faith. One, a woman who had had many twins – all of them thrown away at birth (because it was considered an ill omen) – was one of the converts. One day, Nwoye joined the Christians. On his return, Okonkwo attacked him savagely, until forced to release him by Uchendu. Nwoye that day left his family, never to return. Okonkwo brooded deeply over his bad luck, in having such a disgraceful son.

In the saga of Okonkwo's tragic mistakes, his mishandling of Nwoye's conversion might seem like a slight incident. Yet, like the slaying of Ikemefuna (to which it is, incidentally, casually related – in terms of Nwoye's disenchantment), and the exile in Mbanta (again a destabilising factor for the boy), it is linked to Okonkwo's fatal pride. Theoretically, Okonkwo had the option of responding more understandingly to Nwoye's interest in Christianity. If he had been a wiser man, he might have tolerated it, and thus kept his son. But for Okonkwo, who thinks in simple terms, the boy's defection is simply an abomination, and proof of his (Okonkwo's) bad luck (not proof of his hastiness and bad temper).

Chapter 18

The new church in Mbanta endured a number of crises. The first was their admission of the *osu* (outcasts) of the village. At first the other converts wanted the missionary, Mr Kiaga, to exclude the *osu*, but he argued that they were all children of God. He instructed the outcasts to shave their long hair and clean themselves.

Another crisis was the slaying of the royal python – a sacred snake highly revered by the villagers. This caused great consternation. Finally, after great debate, the elders decided to outlaw all the converts – preventing them from using the stream, the quarry or the market. This crisis was adverted however when the man who killed the python mysteriously died. At that point, the clan relaxed its stand.

While we must tread delicately, and avoid concluding that Achebe is 'putting down' the indigenous culture, it must be acknowledged (again) that

Christianity, at least in the interpretation of the far-sighted and kindly Mr Kiaga, has something to recommend it. The missionary's taking in of the unfortunate *osu* is indeed a charitable act, and very much in the true spirit of Christianity. In accepting Christian teaching on this point, the other converts are in fact behaving in a way we might well approve.

Yet, lest we go too far and re-assess things completely in favour of the missionaries, let us note Mr Kiaga's proud words: 'The heathen speak nothing but falsehood. Only the word of our God is true.' We by now know enough about Ibo culture to know this is simply not true. The subtle point being made by Achebe seems to be this: the difficulty with the missionaries was not that they were promoting a bad religion, but that they assumed theirs was right in every way, and the local faith completely wrong. This European arrogance, not any inherent wrong in European ways, was to prove the greatest danger to indigenous people as the juggernaut of colonialisation rolled over Africa.

Chapter 19

The seven years of exile for Okonkwo are drawing to an end. He asks for huts to be built back in his own home village. Then, with his wives, he prepares a great feast to show his gratitude to his mother's people. At the end of the feast, one of his elderly relatives makes a speech expressing gratitude to Okonkwo, and pointing out that he still does things in the old way – whereas the younger generation are losing touch and a sense of the importance of kinship. The old man refers to the 'abominable religion' that has settled in their midst.

The old man's speech at the end of this chapter (and section) is a cry from the heart of the old (pre-colonial) Africa. It is important to read this for what it tells us about the indigenous point of view – and *not* to dismiss it as a silly old man's ramblings.

There is no doubting that the white man's culture, even at its most benign (Christianity) was enormously disruptive of the local culture. From the Ibo point of view (and to be true to the text we must stay with them, not judge for our own perspective), the schism Europeanisation caused was a terrible thing. Here was an alien force which caused a kind of madness in the community: 'A man can now leave his fathers and his brothers. He can curse the gods of his fathers and his ancestors, like a hunter's dog that suddenly goes mad and turns on his master'. The absolute primacy of 'kinship' (family and clan) has been thrown away (the old man argues), opening up the way to chaos. 'I fear for you [the rest of the clan]', he ends. We remember the Oracle (of Abame) who predicted that the strangers would 'break [the] clan and spread destruction', and note that in a sense it is beginning to come true.

As we end this section, and look back, we realise that the mood has changed quite significantly. Gone is the relative serenity of Section 1, to be replaced by a note of agitation, if not fear. The coming of the white man is only in its early stages, and already the dislocation is considerable.

PART THREE

Chapter 20

Okonkwo returns to his own village with a mixture of apprehension and delight. He has instructed his beautiful young daughters not to marry until they return to their homeland. He calls his sons to him and tells them that he has cast out their brother, Nwoye, for the 'abomination' of deserting his people for the new religion.

Okonkwo is brought up to date with all the things that have been happening since the coming of the white man. A District Commissioner now rules the province, and, aided by *kotma* (native policemen), administers a justice system and a prison for Ibo who break the white man's laws. Okonkwo can't believe that his people have given up without a fight. His friend Obierika tells him that it is 'already too late' – because the white man came 'quietly and peaceably with his religion', insinuating himself into the community, and now, because of the black people who have joined him, it is impossible to get rid of him. Okonkwo hears about one man, Aneto, who killed another over a land dispute and was hung for his offence. Okonkwo is horrified.

By now, we have had some experience seeing the events in the story from different points of view. Simple judgements are difficult. The coming of the white man is bad from the viewpoint of Okonkwo (who was comfortable in his old warrior ways). Yet when we read that he has disowned Nwoye (who has become a 'woman') we naturally feel some uneasiness, and recognise that Okonkwo's way is not without fault. When we read that Okonkwo is horrified that a murder related to land resulted in the offender being hanged, we are subject to quite a lot of cultural confusion. Murder is surely wrong (so we find ourselves distanced from Okonkwo, and his principles). Yet surely hanging is too severe a punishment (putting the white justice system into doubt).

To ask 'Who is right and who is wrong?' is to ask an inappropriate question. Achebe is not inviting us to be judge and jury, but to notice how profoundly destabilising colonisation was. The culture clash involved was massively stressful for all involved.

Chapter 21

Okonkwo is disappointed to find that his return to Umuofia has not created the stir he had anticipated. The people of the clan are preoccupied with the changes brought by the white man. There is not only a government, courts and prison, but also a trading store. The economy has boomed. Mr Brown, the white missionary (and a shrewd judge of character), has treated the local people with respect and in turn been treated well. He has had long talks about religion with a village elder, and knows enough about the people's religion to know that it is strong. Thus he gains the people's confidence by running the school and hospital. His education system is seen to work. Eventually however, due to overwork and ill health, he has to return to England.

The very first sentence of the chapter reminds us that Okonkwo is not in fact representative of all Africans at the point of white colonisation. His unyielding antipathy to the white man and his ways is inspired by a nostalgia for the old, 'warlike' ways, and part of his contempt for anything that could be seen as being 'soft like women'. Others, less belligerent and 'macho' in their thinking, come to find many European innovations (like schooling, and western-style scientifically-based medicine) useful. The white man is often enlightened. Mr Brown, a shrewd and compassionate man, is the benign face of colonisation. Again we see the two sides of the issue.

Chapter 22

Mr Brown's successor is a different kind of man. Reverend James Smith 'saw things as black and white', and takes a very severe line. One day, a particularly zealous convert, Enoch, unmasks one of the *egwugwu* (ancestral spirits), to the horror of all. That night, the *egwugwu* come to seek revenge. First they totally destroy Enoch's compound. Then they approach the church. They are confronted by Mr Smith and his interpreter. They surround him. They tell him that they will not harm him, out of respect for his brother (Mr Brown), but that they will destroy the 'shrine' (church) which has 'bred untold abominations'. They totally destroy the church.

It is all very well for us to acknowledge the good intentions of someone like Mr Brown, but Achebe moves on rapidly to the more dangerous influence of a hard-liner like Smith. Without the earlier man's cultural sensitivity, the clash becomes a dangerous one. Although the punishment meted out on Enoch and Mr Smith is a harsh one, we might in passing note the restraint of the clan elders. They are still capable of much more wisdom than the white man: 'We say he is foolish because he does not know our ways, and perhaps he says we are foolish because we do not know his. Let him go away.'

We must note a line which is so haunting that it is worth drawing attention to. The night after Enoch's sacrilege, 'the very soul of the tribe wept for a great evil that was coming – its own death.' This is one of the rare moments in the text when we hear the author making a point directly – showing that an incident like this is really symbolic of the larger tragedy of colonisation.

Chapter 23

When the District Commissioner returns, Reverend Smith immediately complains to him about what has happened. The Commissioner calls the six leaders of Umuofia to him. On the pretext of having his own people hear their story, he brings in armed men, who imprison the leaders. He tells them that he will not allow anyone to mistreat others, and that they must pay a fine (200 bags of cowries) before they can be released. After he goes, the 'messengers' (kotma) mistreat the elders shamefully. Back in the villages, word spreads about this humiliating development, and the possibility of the men being hanged. In Umuofia, the remaining people gather anxiously and decide to pay the fine.

Events are now escalating rapidly. Despite the relative restraint of the elders (in not killing either Enoch or Mr Smith – as they might have done according to traditional law), and despite the Commissioner's pretence that he will hear their story, things go badly against them. In a heavy-handed display of white arrogance, the Commissioner ignores their viewpoint, simply siding with the white missionary and humiliating the indigenous people who have offended him. The messengers (not members of the tribe, but outsiders not bound by respect for the elders) make matters worse.

It is interesting to examine our responses at this point. With whom do we empathise? The Commissioner or the prisoners? Undoubtedly, most readers would say: the prisoners. This is the payoff for the long introductory section of the novel. Because we can feel for these people, and do not simply indulge in a knee-jerk identification with the white man, the terrible injustice of what is happening strikes us forcibly. That is Achebe's whole point. There is no editorialising – no lectures on colonisation – just the evidence of our feelings for these people. And by now we suspect that the worst is yet to come.

Chapter 24

After the payment of the fine, Okonkwo and the other prisoners are released. Miserably, they make their way back to Umuofia. Despite the food brought by Ezinma, Okonkwo is inconsolable. He cannot sleep, thinking only of vengeance.

The next day there is a great meeting of all the clan in the village square. Okika, the clan orator, tells the people 'all our gods are weeping'. He tells them that they must fight, even if it means killing a clansman (a convert). At this moment, five of the government messengers appear. The leader orders the meeting to cease. Furious, Okonkwo draws his matchet, and beheads the man. The clan meeting breaks up in disarray.

Notice how Okika uses the language of moral righteousness in his speech. 'We must root out this evil,' he says. The 'evil' is the breaking up of the clan, as well as the 'shameful sacrilege' of what happened to the *egwugwu*. Considered from *their* point of view, this is an apt summation, however different it may be from our western perceptions. The warlike response is understandable in their cultural tradition, however different to our way of dealing with problems.

But what happens next is the beginning of the tragedy we have been half expecting. Okonkwo, provoked by his hurt pride and his overwhelming sense of grievance, takes the warrior way, when the clan meeting is contemptuously interrupted by government messengers. The killing of the messenger is clearly a disaster. We know what happened to Aneto (Chapter 20), and therefore where that leaves Okonkwo. He is trapped, a victim of his own anger, and more broadly, of a political force far bigger than he is. We can only now await what must be the bitter end of the story.

Chapter 25

The District Commissioner, surrounded by armed men, arrives at the village. He asks the assembled villagers where Okonkwo is. They lead the way. Okonkwo's body is hanging from a tree in the bush behind his compound.

Obierika, Okonkwo's friend, protests at the way the white man 'drove him to kill himself'. But all the Commissioner can think about is the paragraph he will devote to 'this man' in his forthcoming book – *The Pacification of the Primitive Tribes of the Lower Niger.*

It is worth noting how explosive this climax is. After such a long and leisurely first section, the novel has built up enormous narrative energy. The ominous signs have been there for some time, but even so the shock of the conclusion (Chapters 24 and 25) is formidable. We may have had our reservations about Okonkwo as a person, but we cannot help feeling something of the grief of Obierika (and guessing at the trauma for the dead man's family).

Indeed we see suddenly the whole tragic arc of Okonkwo's story: 'one of the greatest men in Umuofia' brought low (as Obierika quite rightly sees it) by his enemy. Knowing full well that he has committed an act that will result in his death, Okonkwo has taken his own life, rather than be further humiliated by his enemy. But in doing so, he has broken his own culture's taboo (on suicide). Mighty indeed is his fall, for this once great man 'will now be buried like a dog'.

While Okonkwo's case is an extreme one (as the author has implicitly acknowledged), somehow the whole tragedy of white colonisation is summed up symbolically in what has happened. In case we miss the point, note how the perspective switches in the novel's last paragraph. Suddenly we are reading the thoughts of the Commissioner. The 'conqueror' has taken over, effectively hijacking the narrative voice of the text at its very end. The white man knows nothing of Okonkwo ('this man') and doesn't care. He is only 'interesting' to the Commissioner as an example of 'primitive' people, who did not always readily accept their 'pacification' (a white euphemism for subjugation). We, however, who have known Okonkwo and his people intimately, are moved to take a different view, *dissenting* from this emblematic white man and seeing instead the whole tragedy of what happened in Africa (from the indigenous point of view). As one critic summed it up:

> In the very last paragraph of the novel, the narrative perspective shifts to that of the British District Commissioner...This shift signals the collapse of the traditional viewpoint that has authorised the story so far. And the District Commissioner regards this tragic episode simply as material to be included in a book he hopes to write...This shift comes as a shock, and that shock reveals the magnitude of Achebe's achievement. The inadequacy of that colonial officer's perspective is palpable to any reader. These were no tribes in need of pacification; they were a dignifieid, culturally rich, politically self-sufficient society in no need of British rule. (R.D.Dasenbrock, *Salmagundi*, Nos 68 & 69, 1985-6)

The author does not tell us what to think or feel. We have been positioned with masterly skill. The story says it all.

NOTES ON
CHARACTERS, THEMES AND ISSUES

CHARACTERS

Okonkwo

O konkwo functions in the text both as a character in his own right, and as an emblem of what happened to all Africans under white colonisation. We will consider these two strands in turn.

As an individual, Okonkwo is quite clearly drawn. Achebe never whitewashes his central character, nor does he condemn him. We are aware of both sides of his personality – the noble achiever (see particularly the first several chapters), the brave, self-reliant warrior – and the impetuous, intemperate man who unwittingly courts disaster. We see the solid family man and we see the wife beater. We understand that he genuinely loves people like Ekwefi and Ezinma, yet cannot bring himself to show it.

To some extent, Okonkwo's strengths are also his weaknesses. His pride and adherence to the old warrior code are what finally condemns him to death. Doubtless Okonkwo sums up for the author both the positive attributes and the limitations of many pre-colonial African men – warlike and courageous within the context of their traditional lifestyle, or if we can put it in sociobiological terms, well adapted to their environment – but seriously maladapted to the new, westernised lifestyle.

In analysing his character, it is important for us to acknowledge the good things (for he is not really very likeable, for the most part). He is a 'self-made man', who started with nothing, and by hard work, courage and dogged persistence became 'one of the greatest men'. We understand his need for self-esteem (or putting it another way, the need to avoid the humiliation his father suffered), his wish to be respected. It is a universal human trait. While the culture (and the warrior aspects) may be alien to us, the urge for 'greatness' (dignity, honour) is not.

That is the positive side. Then there are his faults. Among the comments about Okonkwo, we might well remember particularly these:

'He had no patience with unsuccessful men.' (Chapter 1)

'He threw himself into [becoming a wealthy and important man] like one possessed. And indeed he was possessed, by the fear of his father's contemptible life and shameful death.' (Chapter 3)

'Okonkwo never showed any emotion openly, unless it be the emotion of anger. To show affection was a sign of weakness.' (Chapter 4)

'Okonkwo was not a man of thought but of action.' (Chapter 8)

One of the saddest passages in the whole novel is this one:

He heard Ikemefuna cry, 'My father, they have killed me!' as he ran towards him. Dazed with fear, Okonkwo drew his matchet and cut him down. He was afraid of being thought weak. (Chapter 7)

His need for pride and masculine affirmation verge on the obsessive, and slip easily into aggression and insensitivity. Most European readers squirm when they read about the beatings he gives Ekwefi, Nwoye and others. It is no accident that Achebe shows us these aspects of his nature. They are the dark side of the man, and part of his problem.

Perhaps it helps to think in terms of an analogy. He is like a league footballer who is revered on the field as a 'tough guy', but cannot have proper relationships with his children because of this very toughness. Or a brilliant businessman who starts out penniless and ends up a multi-millionaire, only to find his compulsive work habits and broken relationships have ruined his enjoyment of life.

Like so many tragic heroes, Okonkwo is basically a good man, but with fatal flaws. His pride, his ambition, his love of being a warrior – all 'good' things within the context of his traditional culture – combine to ruin him. And he doesn't even understand what happened. He can't see that his own personality has provoked the fatal collision with the white man. Having taken action (as he feels he must to be a 'man'), he finds he is (or will be) condemned to death, and so takes his life, which has become (in his view) intolerable anyway. It is a long established narrative pattern, going right back to the ancient Greeks. But it is still just as sad, and just as instructive.

The other thread in Okonkwo's role in the novel is the emblematic one. While Achebe never suggests that the circumstances of Okonkwo's fate match that of indigenous people generally, he allows us to feel that a symbolic 'death' is involved with the coming of the white man. The death of the old ways, the death of the clan, the loss of pride, the loss of meaning – all are simultaneously present both in what happens to Okonkwo and what happens to the wider native population. That is made abundantly clear not only in several speeches about the 'abomination' of the new ways (see Chapters 19 and 24 particularly), but in the final paragraph of the novel, where the District Commissioner writes off the protagonist in a few words, seeing him as just a case study in 'pacification'. As suggested above, the shock of the ending has a double edge – it is both the dead body of Okonkwo that we contemplate, and the death of the old, authentic, indigenous Africa.

Ekwefi

Most of Okonkwo's wives and children are not even named. They are merely background characters whose presence is referred to but not detailed in any meaningful way. Ekwefi and her daughter Ezinma are significant exceptions.

Ekwefi is quite a well developed character, though she takes centre stage in only five chapters (5,6,9,11,12), and isn't even mentioned at the end. She is a strong woman, who knows what she wants, and speaks her mind. We know that she left her first husband, to whom she had been joined in an arranged marriage, and married Okonkwo for love (see the end of Chapter 11). She loves his masculine qualities – his prowess as a wrestler, his strength and success – which to her are obviously great merits, even though she is once or twice on the receiving end of his wrath. Though a traditional Ibo woman, whose obedience to her husband is beyond question, she has qualities we might recognise in modern western women too.

We also feel for her in her unhappiness – particularly her despair at losing so many children, and her heart-breaking terror at the possibility that the fever will claim Ezinma too. The tragedy of lost loved ones is one that transcends (and unites) all cultures.

It is important for readers to identify with one of the

protagonist's wives. People like Ekwefi fill in the texture of the culture a little more, and help us bridge the gap to that time and place. Okonkwo alone is not a sufficient tie, given the problematic nature of his personality. In seeing how life was for someone like Ekwefi, we see a little more of what was lost in the transition from traditional culture, if perhaps also what was gained.

Ezinma

The irony is that Ezinma, Okonkwo's favourite child, has more of the 'gutsy' qualities that he likes than any of his sons. Although she struggled through childhood, she grows up a beautiful and spirited young woman, to his delight. It is a small part of his tragedy that he does not live to see her married, another of his proud projects.

Ezinma is actually a bridge between readers and Okonkwo in her own right. She is the one who understands him, despite his bluster and tough exterior, seeing the more kindly man beneath the warrior front. She is the one who tries to comfort him and get him to eat after the terrible humiliation of the imprisonment. In seeing her love for him, we recognise something that could easily have been lost in the general impression we have of him as a 'tough guy'. When we contemplate his death at the conclusion of the story, our feelings must be coloured by our understanding of what someone like Ezinma would feel at seeing her father's inglorious end. For her, as well as for Obierika, Ekwefi and unnamed others, it is truly a tragedy.

Nwoye

Nwoye is a character in his own right, as well as a 'counter argument' of kinds.

Quiet, sensitive, unsuited by temperament to the harsh warrior culture of his father, he suffers considerably from the gap between what Okonkwo expects, and what Nwoye is able to deliver. He tries in vain to go along with his father's principles. We read that he 'knew it was right to be masculine and to be violent, but somehow he still preferred the stories that his mother used to tell'. He is privately appalled by the abandonment of twins, and traumatised by the death of his childhood companion Ikemefuna (at Okonkwo's own hands). Nwoye himself experiences a 'culture clash' long before the white man comes, and he finds an alternative.

With the coming of Christianity, Nwoye is relieved to find an ideology more in keeping with his own nature. 'He felt a relief within as the hymn poured into his parched soul,' we read. He is an early convert to the new faith, which accords with his own far more compassionate bent.

It is at this point that we have to concede that Nwoye is also a counter-argument within the predominantly anti-colonial scheme of the novel. Not all aspects of westernisation were bad, hints the author. For Nwoye (as for Achebe's own father, we know), the new ways were a way out of 'darkness', as well as a loss. Achebe has carefully positioned Nwoye as a reminder that a too hasty polarisation (Ibo good, white man bad) is not true to the complexities of what really happened, and what he wants to show us in his text.

Obierika

To Obierika falls the duty of Okonkwo's obituary. It is a simple one, as befits this simple but perceptive individual: 'This man was one of the greatest men in Umuofia. You drove him to kill himself; and now he will be buried like a dog.'

Obierika is not particularly well defined as a character, but that doesn't really matter. His role, beyond fleshing out our sense of what the indigenous Africans were like (not all as aggessive as Okonkwo), is to be the mouthpiece of 'the clan' when Okonkwo dies. We ought to note that after his outburst (the words above), Obierika cannot speak. Though a warrior, he is choked with emotion – for he sees not just the cruel and unnecessary death of his friend, but the desecration of the land (and by implication the destruction of all that he holds dear). His is the last Ibo voice we hear in the book, and thus his words have even more importance. After him come just the messengers and the District Commissioner, and theirs are the voices of aliens.

The District Commissioner

The DC is not even named. He is without interest as a character, but is highly significant as a type (or representative figure). He is the face of the British colonial system – shrewd, manipulative, arrogant, proud of its 'civilising' function and its Christian ethics, but at heart empty of compassion and in a sense immoral.

The final words of the novel belong to the Commissioner, as remarked above, because he is the face and voice of the conqueror. He looks at a man who has hung himself in disgrace. He hears that this was one of the 'greatest' among the subjugated people. Unmoved, he mentally files the incident to become part of his self-congratulatory memoirs. Thus it was (Achebe implies) with the whole colonial movement (in Nigeria and elsewhere). The local people were not individuals, human beings with their own names and lives, but 'details' within the grand scheme of 'pacification' of Africa. Achebe does not need to make the Commissioner a monster. His very ordinariness, his bureaucratic indifference, is both more plausible and more chilling.

THEMES

The tragedy of colonisation

Turning and turning in the widening gyre
The falcon cannot hear the falconer;
Things fall apart; the centre cannot hold;
Mere anarchy is loosed upon the world. (Prefatory quote)

At first glance, *Things Fall Apart* appears to be about Okonkwo. In fact its real subject is much larger. As one critic wrote:

The theme of the novel is stated clearly on page 160: 'He has put a knife on the things that held us together and we have fallen apart.' With the arrival of the white man and his new religion and administration, traditional society's cracks and weaknesses, hitherto concealed by the common fear of the ancestors and the gods, breaks open and the once-stable community collapses. (Eustace Palmer, *Africana*, 1972)

Achebe is showing the 'fall' of a man, but also the fall of a people. While he takes pains not to idealise the old ways, and acknowledges that the coming of white men was not all bad, the overwhelming feeling at the end is of sadness (if not tragedy).

The tragedy of colonisation is what gives the novel its name. Achebe has borrowed three words from the famous Irish poet W.B.Yeats (quoted above). Here are the following lines in the poem.

The blood-dimmed tide is loosed, and everywhere
The ceremony of innocence is drowned;
The best lack all conviction, while the worst
Are full of passionate intensity.

The Second Coming (1921) was written just after the chaos of the First World War, and it expresses profound despair. If we apply the poem to Achebe's novel, we see that he is indeed depicting 'anarchy loosed upon the world' (of the Ibo). We might read the circling falcon as the young Ibo (like Nwoye) and the falconer as the elders whom they cannot (or will not) hear; the ceremonies (of the old culture) could be said to be 'drowned'; a 'blood dimmed tide' is loosed, and 'the best' (perhaps the best of the indigenous people) have lost conviction, while the worst (like the 'messengers') gain the ascendancy.

If we consider what damage the white invasion does, we would have to mention the beginning of the end for the old religion (the 'false gods' whom the missionaries attack), the breaking down of family and kinship ties (something clearly evident in the case of Nwoye), the supplanting of native cultural systems (justice, respect for ancestral spirits, etc), and above all the massive loss of self-esteem amongst the indigenous people. The imprisonment of the *egwugwu* is a case in point. They are humiliated by the white Commissioner, and then abused by the alien kotma. It is this profound loss of face which leads to Okonkwo's outburst, and the novel's tragic climax.

A major reason why *Things Fall Apart* is considered so important a work is that, while its reference point is Africa, in fact it sums up well what things were like for indigenous people in countries round the world. There is now a considerable body of anti-colonial literature, but Achebe's landmark 1958 novel remains a key text. The cultural and psychological trauma of what happened to Okonkwo's people was replicated for millions of 'primitive tribes' in Africa, the

Americas, Asia and of course Australia – as white Europeans took possession of and imposed their alien ways on new lands. The consequences of those invasions are still being felt around the world.

The tragedy of pride

'The oldest man present said sternly that those whose palm-kernels were cracked for them by a benevolent spirit should not forget to be humble.' (Of Okonkwo, Chapter 4)

One common reading of *Things Fall Apart* is to see it as the tragedy of a man whose pride and intransigence ruin him. This is a variation of the classical Greek formula, as seen in works like *Medea*, and later in the tragedies of Shakespeare (*Macbeth*, *Hamlet*, etc). The formula, put simply, is that a great man falls because of some inner weakness (usually called the 'tragic flaw') which, despite his basically good intentions, is his undoing.

In this interpretation, Okonkwo suffers from exaggerated pride at his own achievements, combined with an overly aggressive personality. His pride is quite clearly motivated. We know how humiliated he was by his own father's 'shameful' (read, inglorious, underachieving) life, and how this inferiority complex pushed him into what we might call over-compensation. Repeatedly, we read about his arrogance, both in explicit authorial comments ('He had no patience with unsuccessful men' and 'His life had been ruled by a great passion – to become one of the lords of the clan') and in the subtext of his behaviour (eg. when he scorns other, lesser men – as at the beginning Chapter 4). And of course the action which triggers his death is quintessentially a result of pride. The messenger has ordered them to stop the meeting. Okonkwo doesn't sulk, he doesn't yell, he doesn't fight. He kills the man on the spot, hitting back (at what he perceives as a personal as well as communal insult) out of his own humiliation (hurt pride) and anger.

That the issue of pride might have some larger ethical dimension, and be symbolically linked (in the classical manner) to his tragedy, is signalled in the text by the three 'sins' Okonkwo commits against the gods: first, breaking the Week of Peace (when he beats Ekwefi); second, killing Ikemefuna (when he has been specifically warned to have no hand in the boy's death); third, killing the son of Ezeudu (an accident, but related to his aggressiveness, and somehow symbolic). Like classic tragic heroes, whose pride was seen as a defiance of the gods, and whose fall was read as divine 'punishment' for their 'sins', Okonkwo's story submits to the interpretation that his arrogance precipitates his tragic end.

In fairness, it should be added that alternative interpretations exist, in particular the view that he is not really responsible, but merely a victim of overwhelming outside forces. However, the 'classical' reading of his fall is an important possibility, and well worth considering.

The challenge of cultural difference

'All their customs are upside-down. They do not decide on bride-price as we do, with sticks. They haggle and bargain as if they were buying a goat or a cow in the market.'
'That is very bad,' said Obierika's eldest brother. 'But what is good in one place is bad in another place.'

It may seem laughable to read about African tribesmen thinking other tribes' methods of fixing a 'bride-price' ridiculous, when we regard a bride-price itself as worse than ridiculous. Yet this example is only one of many such challenges posed by the novel to our broad-mindedness and ability to transcend cultural differences. Depending on a particular reader's sensibilities, the treatment of women in this traditional society might be the sticking point, or the thowing away of twins, or the mutilation of stillborn children – and the list goes on.

As the above quote makes plain, Achebe is very much aware of this issue. Furthermore, as has been pointed out by various commentators, he is as interested in the cultural interaction between white men and the traditional people of Africa as he is in the colonial or 'cultural destruction' theme. Consider for instance the quite lengthy passage in Chapter 21 devoted to the discussion between Mr Brown and Akunna (the village elder) about the differences between Christianity and the Ibo religion.

It is possible to break the characters down into two groups with respect to this theme: the culturally open-minded and tolerant (Mr

Brown, Nwoye, Okeke) and the narrow-minded (Okonkwo, Reverend Smith, the DC). We should acknowledge that both black and white are represented in both categories!

When we consider our own context, as readers, we would probably have to admit that this division is repeated. There are those who interpret culturally different people and customs in a sympathetic manner, trying to 'walk in other people's shoes' (to quote the famous novel about racial tolerance, *To Kill a Mockingbird*), rather than make snap judgements based on prejudice. And there are those who consider their own ways of doing things self-evidently correct, and all alternatives inferior, if not downright 'wrong'.

One of the beauties of *Things Fall Apart* is the way it forces us to see things from the point of view of very different people. Achebe is not forcing us to agree with everything the Ibo do, but he is equally not inviting us to see them as unrelievedly bad. The novel implicitly argues for cultural tolerance, and the recognition of both good and bad aspects in all cultures.

The universality of human experience

'A man's life from birth to death was a series of transition rites which brought him nearer and nearer to his ancestors.'

Beneath apparent differences, much remains the same, the world over. While perhaps it takes a little getting used to the initial strangeness of Ibo ways, the novel only works because we recognise in those people things we experience in our own lives. Let us consider some obvious examples.

There is Ekwefi's misery at the thought of losing her only daughter, Ezinma – exactly like the fear of any parent for a sickly child. There is Okonkwo's pride in his grown up daughters, and his disgust at the son (Nwoye) who didn't follow in his father's footsteps. There is, to consider the other side of that equation, Nwoye's problem dealing with an authoritarian and undemonstrative father, and his all too predictable rebellion. There is Okonkwo's lament when he is forced by an accident to go into exile, and his wretchedness at his loss of status. The speech made by Uchendu about suffering could have been made in any culture, for it is a universal theme. Turning to more political issues, we note the way the Christian evangelists 'sell' their new religion to their would-be converts, the way the messengers (of the white authorities), draw power from their role (not unlike modern bureaucrats), the way they 'rip off' the system. None of these patterns is at all specific to Africa. Each one is to be found in contemporary western society. Only the clothes and language differ.

Common threads exist not only in the social and psychological detail, but in the broader and symbolic patterns of the text. These notes have already remarked on the central theme of (Okonkwo's) dangerous pride. It is a standard theme of literature the world over. The ancient Greeks called it 'hubris' and made it the central mechanism of their great tragedies. The Hebrews saw it as the root cause of the 'fall of man' (from the *Garden of Eden*). The Christians made it the cardinal 'sin' and urged humility in the sight of God ('The meek shall inherit the Earth'). So when we identify it as the major source of Okonkwo's problems (he is warned as early as Chapter 4 that 'he should not forget to be humble'), we know we are seeing something that is age old and universal.

Achebe achieves a highly specific sense of time and place. He also achieves a type of universality, showing that the human experience of people in Africa a century ago is in so many ways, beyond the surface detail, remarkably similar to that in our own age, and all times.

Change, entropy, suffering

'For whom is it well, for whom is it well?
There is no one for whom it is well.'
(Uchendu, quoting a traditional Ibo song)

One of the most problematical aspects of *Things Fall Apart* is the complexity of Achebe's attitude towards the past. As mentioned already, he refuses to simply glorify the old ways of pre-colonial Africa, no matter how sympathetically he may render them. Achebe himself has written:

The credibility of the world [an African writer] is attempting to recreate will be called into question and he will defeat his own purpose if he is suspected of glossing over the inconvenient facts. We cannot pretend that our past was one long, technicolour idyll. We have to admit that like other people's pasts ours had its good as well as its bad sides. (quoted in Prafulla Kar's 'The Image of the Vanishing African in Chinua Achebe's Novels', *The Colonial and the Neo-Colonial Encounters in Commonwealth Literature*, University of Mysore, 1983)

If the transition from traditional culture to a British-dominated colonial regime was neither totally good nor all bad, then what is Achebe saying? It is possible to argue that his interest is in the nature of *change* itself.

Okonkwo's tragedy springs from his refusal to compromise with the change that is slowly coming over Africa....The [move from a decentralised, tribal society to a centralised, Europeanised society], Achebe seems to suggest, represents an inevitable movement of history, and when Okonkwo refuses to accept the Christian missionaries and the British administration, he, in a way, obstructs the flow of history and, in the process, is swallowed. His tragedy...stems from his refusal to "grow", to lose his "innocence" in the "rite of passage". (Prafulla Kar's essay, cited above)

Change would on the face of it appear to be a neutral issue, but in Okonkwo's case it is definitely for the worse. Other critics have noted the predominantly tragic cast of Achebe's writing (in general), and his tendency to see suffering as central to the human condition. *Things Fall Apart* certainly submits to this interpretation too. The twin focal points of the novel are the 'fall' of Okonkwo, and behind him the 'fall' of indigenous Africans in general. Throughout there are hints that death and disgrace, flood and drought – in short all manner of trials – are a constant in human life. 'Entropy' – the natural tendency of things to 'run down' over time – is several times implied. Suffering is much in evidence. The Uchandu quote given above is strangely reminiscent of the ancient Greek maxim (from Sophocles' famous play *Oedipus Rex*): 'Count no man happy until he is dead'.

What is one to do in the face of change, dissolution and suffering? Uchendu sums it up in his speech (Chapter 14). One endures. One moves with the times. One finds the pleasures in life, and tries not to 'allow sorrow to weigh you down and kill you'. And if one doesn't, like Okonkwo, then it is all over – pleasure and pain – too soon.

WHAT THE CRITICS SAY

Mr Achebe is a young Nigerian. In *Things Fall Apart*, his first novel, he draws a fascinating picture of tribal life among his own people at the end of the nineteenth century. His literary method is apparently simple, but a vivid imagination illuminates every page, and his style is a model of clarity...

The great interest of this novel is that it genuinely succeeds in presenting tribal life from the inside. Patterns of feeling and attitudes of mind appear clothed in a distinctively African imagery, written neither up nor down...

Only at the end of the book, when the European missionaries appear on the scene, does some confusion of attitude prevail. For Mr Achebe himself owes much to missionary education, and his sympathies are naturally more with the new than the old. His picture of the collapse of tribal custom is perhaps less than compassionate.

(The Times Literary Supplement, No. 2938, June 20, 1958)

Writing with admirable detachment, [Achebe] creates in the central character, Okonkwo, a great literary figure... a powerful and ambitious man whose faithfulness to the importance of order is so strong that we might say his destruction comes from this strength rather [than] from any weakness.

As if to impact on us what is lost in the Okonkwo story, Achebe at first focuses on the closely circumscribed arena of the village, so that until the final quarter of the novel there is no real sense that a 'world' exists anywhere outside the village. Okonkwo, hard and unbending in his attachment to this tribal life, which is all he knows, goes down to his destruction with all the inevitability of an Oedipus.

(Robert McDowell, *Studies in Black Literature*, Vol 2, No 1, Spring, 1971)

The language of Achebe's novels presents a highly skilful hand. He has a wonderful, true ear for Nigerian and English speech rhythms and a simple-seeming but very sophisticated use of metaphor. He has understood and mastered, and made it a dominant feature of his writing, the English philosophy of understatement and it concomitant bare narrative style. And much of his narrative style has its roots in a very wide literary tradition. The writings of many nations have been concerned with the effects of dramatic change on traditional ways of life.....Themes in literature are rarely original. It is in their individual treatment that they take on their own particular colouration. Achebe's novels define not only situations common to the Old Icelandic Sagas but ones which recur in much of modern literature. Because he places them in his own environment, which although, specifically Nigerian, is still a microcosm of a much larger world, he gives to them a fresh colour and insight.

(Kate Turkington, *English Studies in Africa*, Vol 14, No. 2, September, 1971)

[*Things Fall Apart*] is a short and extraordinarily close-knit novel which in fictional terms creates the way of life of an Ibo village community when white missionaries and officials were first penetrating Eastern Nigeria. The highly selective details with which Achebe represents the seasonal festivals and ceremonies, the religion, social customs, and political structure of an Ibo village create the vivid impression of a complex, self-sufficient culture seemingly able to deal in traditional ways with any challenge that nature and human experience might fling at it...[The] greatest strength of *Things Fall Apart* is the tragic 'objectivity' with which Achebe handles a dual theme. There are two main, closely intertwined tragedies – the personal tragedy of Okonkwo, 'one of the greatest men in Umuofia', and the public tragedy of the eclipse of one culture by another.

Things Fall Apart is impressive for the wide range of what it so pithily covers, for the African flavour of scene and language, but above all the way in which Achebe makes that language the instrument for analysing tragic experience and profound human issues of very much more that local Nigerian significance....

(Arthur Ravenscroft, *Chinua Achebe,* Longman, 1969)

Achebe's *Things Fall Apart*, which appeared in 1958, was the first West African novel in English which could be applauded without reserve....

[*Things Fall Apart*] is an extremely well-constructed short novel, fully equal to its theme and written with confidence and precision. Achebe's theme is suggested in the Yeatsian title, but although he sees the disintegration of the Ibo society as a communal and personal tragedy for those who lived through it, this does not in any way obscure his objectivity in describing that society as it was....

Achebe's brief, almost laconic style, his refusal to justify, explain or condemn, are responsible for a good deal of the book's success. The novelist presents to us a picture of traditional Ibo life as just as he can make it. The final judgement of that life, as of the life which replaced it, is left to us. Only Achebe insists that we should see it as a life actually lived by plausible men and women before we dismiss it, with the usual shrug, as nothing but ignorance, darkness and death. His people win, and deservedly win, our full respect as individuals whose life had dignity, significance and positive values.

(Gerald Moore, *Seven African Writers*, Oxford University Press, London, 1970)

Chinua Achebe's first novel, *Things Fall Apart* is unquestionably his best. Never again was he to demonstrate such mastery of plot construction, such keen psychological insight, and such an ability to hold his themes steadily before his mind and pursue them convincingly to a logical conclusion. *Things Fall Apart* derives its strength from the quality of the author's perception of the social forces at work in an ancient and proud society, and from his admirable knowledge of human psychology shown in the development of Okonkwo's character. There are distinct affinities between the work of Achebe and that of Hardy. Both show a keen awareness of the movement of social forces and their effort on the destiny of ordinary people.

(Eustace Palmer, *Africana,* 1972)

HSC COURSE NOTES

The following notes explain the way *Things Fall Apart* is being used in the Higher School Certificate, in which it is a reference text for the Area of Study in the ESL course.

AREA OF STUDY: PERSPECTIVE

This area of study explores the ways different perspectives shape understanding of the world. Perspectives are influenced by individuality, personal history and culture. Viewing events from different perspectives can uncover some of these influences and the ways their effects can remain unrecognised or misunderstood. Close language study and experimenting with different language choices assist us to understand the ways language shapes and expresses perceptions.

Defining perspective

'Perspective' is defined in the dictionary as view, apparent relationship, way in which people, ideas or things are perceived, or in common language, ways of seeing things. Do we for example see passing an exam as 'an impossible task', or as 'challenging but doable'? Is a new acquaintance fun and colourful, or brash and tiresome? It's all in *the way we see the thing or person* being considered.

We should be familiar with the terms 'objective', meaning external to the mind, or 'real' (having the quality of an object commonly agreed by everyone to be the same eg the number one or the colour red), and 'subjective', meaning the viewpoint of a particular mind, an *inward* reality, a 'perception' as opposed to a 'fact' (eg too many, 'hot' colour). So physical categories (girl, boy, hot, cold) are normally considered to be objective issues, whereas moral categories (good, bad) are usually thought of as subjective. It depends, as we often say, on your point of view (your perspective). A distinction is normally made in psychology and philosophy between what scientists can prove to be a **fact**, and what people merely believe or feel to be the case (**opinion**).

Perspective (how we see or judge a person or idea) can be a highly individual mix of fact and feeling. For instance, we might think of getting up in front of the school to make a speech as 'very hard' or 'impossible'. Our perspective on this matter might be informed by both the facts of the situation (a speech is a complex text form, I am not all that good at English, to judge by my marks) and by our subjective input (I am scared of failing, I have been unlucky of late). Such perspectives can of course change over time. A Toastmaster course in public speaking would probably change both objective and subjective inputs to our perception that speech-making was difficult.

Reasons for differing perspective

While there are literally dozens of reasons for the different ways people perceive the same things, here are three of the most obvious.

Personality (or individuality)

Personality refers to the individual's emotional makeup. Is she extroverted (outgoing) or introverted (shy and retiring)? Is she nervous or confident, a 'scaredy-cat' or a risk-taker? Is she mostly 'logical' or mostly emotional? Is she tidy and precise, or disorderly and impetuous?

Psychologists tells us that these sorts of basic characteristics come from a mix of **heredity** (ie the genetic blueprint passed on by parents) and **environment**. Children often 'take after' one or both parents, though the extent to which this mimicry is 'wired in' or learned is the subject of unending debate. A temperamental mother who finds it difficult to be affectionate can produce a 'difficult', standoffish son or daughter. Certain kinds of hyperactivity or fearfulness can 'run in families', like diseases. Identical twins raised separately demonstrate remarkable similarities, which points to the power of heredity. Children raised in orphanages tend to be emotionally stunted, which points to the power of environment.

Most theorists tend to agree that the early years lay down the basic patterns for life. Personality is formed, or becomes obvious, in the first five or so years, and thereafter sets up predispositions for the rest of life. A middle child who feels neglected and unloved can quickly become a 'whiner', always demanding attention and feeling that life is somehow unfair. The same person can still be demanding attention decades later, not of its parents but of its own children.

Experience (or personal history)

What happens to a person invariably shapes his or her perceptions. Famous Holocaust survivor Elie Wiesel saw his father perish in Hitler's death camps, and lost his faith in God. An Australian diver shipwrecked three times, the last time losing his mate to sharks, vowed never to go on the water in his life again.

Some experiences can be **traumatic**, and cause negative changes to our view of life ('Life's a bitch'). Other experiences can be **affirming**. The classic case is of people who pray to God for help in a time of crisis, and find their religious faith or belief in the essential goodness of people renewed ('People are basically kind and well meaning').

Beliefs (or culture)

People need 'rules' or patterns to make sense of the world. The most obvious of these are **religious** and **political** beliefs, which offer explanations of why things are as they are, and how people should act. Religion usually states that God rules the world, and that as long as a person obeys God's commands (revealed in 'sacred' books like the Bible or the Koran), all will be well. Politics may claim that free enterprise (capitalism) is the only viable system, because it rewards people for effort, or that all people should share (socialism), because people are basically selfish.

People will interpret situations in the light of their belief systems and act accordingly. For instance, a Catholic girl who gets pregnant accidentally will tend to have the baby because her belief system tells her that abortion is 'murder'.

THE AREA OF STUDY AND THE TEXT

Things Fall Apart says a lot about 'perspective'. The most obvious division in the novel is between the perspective of the Ibo (Okonkwo and his clan) and the British (the District Commissioner, etc).

From Okonkwo's point of view (or perspective), all white people are 'evil'. Their religion is an 'abomination' and their influence pernicious. They come, uninvited, and destroy the clan. In the light of his personal pride (individuality), his personal history (humiliation at his father, which he has redressed by a life of strict assertiveness and achievement) and his culture (which applauds the warrior style and scorns 'weakness'), Okonkwo has no choice but to fight against the white man. That his reaction causes his own death makes complete sense in terms of 'where he is coming from'.

From the point of view of the white men who colonise Africa, Okonkwo and his clan are 'primitive tribes'. The District Commissioner and Reverend Smith see the Ibo as natives to be 'pacified'. We are given few details about the white authorities' individual nature (though we know that Mr Smith thinks in 'black and white') and none about their personal history, but understand their culture well enough to know that it shapes them in a totally different way – giving Christianity the status of the one true religion, exalting European customs and values above anything (no matter how wise or worthy) that is part of Ibo culture. Because we have been privileged by Achebe and know what Ibo culture is like from the inside, we know that the white man's intolerant and contemptuous judgement is ill-founded. Yet, because he is in a position of dominance, he can enforce his perceptions. The way the perspective of the narrative changes in the last chapter of the book (from an Ibo perspective to the DC's) underlines this political aspect. The conquerors write the history. *Their* perspective rules.

Beyond Okonkwo and the Ibo of Nigeria, the novel can be taken to refer to the wider issue of power in the context of colonisation. In Australia, for instance, something very similar happened. After white settlement and the 'paciification' of the Aborigines, it was the white perspective that was privileged. This perspective, notoriously racist and superior, ignored almost entirely the perspective of the indigenous people. The result has been 200 years of misery for the Aborigines, continuing guilt and confusion for white Australians.

The safest line to take in approaching this theme is doubtless to suggest that there is no 'right' perspective – just different perspectives, depending on who you are, and where you come from.

SAMPLE ESSAY (VCE PART 1)

'Okonkwo was a victim of circumstances. His tragedy was due to forces outside his control.'

Do you agree?

'That man was one of the greatest men in Umuofia. You drove him to kill himself; and now he will be buried like a dog...' This cry of outrage, from Okonkwo's best friend, sums up in very strong language the claim that Okonkwo was a victim of circumstances. The melancholy ending of the novel can easily be read as the brutal crushing not only of Okonkwo, but of all indigenous Africans, by the white man. However, was it all the white man's fault? Achebe plants many seeds of doubt about his protagonist, who could also be read as a foolish, headstrong man. Was he a victim, or did he destroy himself?

The victim theory is the easy one to argue. Although Achebe takes care not to idealise the old ways of the Ibo before the coming of the British, he presents overall a very positive picture of traditional life. In the lengthy first section of *Things Fall Apart*, readers are gently introduced to Okonkwo's clan. They read about the weddings, funerals, the feasts and dancing. After what might be initial surprise, they become familiar with the polygamous marriages and the other indigenous customs. They grow to appreciate the rich folklore, the wise justice system, the democratic political style and the largely benign customs of these people. Then suddenly, the colonists invade, and 'things fall apart'. Okonkwo sees his son seduced by the 'abomination' of a new religion. He is horrified when the *egwugwu* are exposed in an act of unthinkable sacrilege. When the elders administer a suitable punishment to the perpetrator, they find themselves imprisoned, and shamed, beyond endurance. The 'evil' white man has taken over his land, and seems bent on making him and his people slaves. It is in this context that he lashes out, dealing the fatal blow against the enemy's messenger that is also his own death sentence. He knows then that a force outside his control will come to crush him, in retaliation for what he has done. Because he cannot tolerate such an end, he takes his own life. In this reading, Okonkwo is the victim. Indeed, he stands for all the indigenous people of colonised territories who were subjugated by Europeans, a vast crime that is still having repercussions.

However, there is another reading. At best, this one casts Okonkwo in the role of tragic hero – at worst, as a fool with a fatally short temper. There are plenty of textual clues. 'He had no patience with unsuccessful men,' we read. He was 'like one possessed...by the fear of his father's contemptible life and shameful death', and, ominously, 'Okonkwo never showed emotion openly, unless it be the emotion of anger'. And there is the deadly 'Okonkwo was not a man of thought but of action'. These signs of his arrogance and impetuousness can be aligned to classical tragedy, not to mention the universal folk wisdom of 'pride going before a fall'. From the trivial, such as when Okonkwo insults a man who has few titles, and has to be be rebuked by an elder for his lack of humility, to the highly important, as when he kills Ikemefuna 'because he was afraid of being thought weak', he can be said to be courting disaster. His fragile sense of manhood, and utter resistance to any change, together with a giant ego, are burdens he carries through life. His rashness arguably was always going to cause him trouble. When the white man arrives, and Okonkwo comes into direct contact with a greater 'enemy' force, catastrophe is almost inevitable. Did the white man drive him to it, or did his own failings unleash the murderous rage that led him to murder and then suicide? All Africans may have been victims, in a sense, but Okonkwo's fate was in this reading largely his own fault.

So which theory provides a best fit with the text? While *Things Fall Apart* positions readers to be deeply sympathetic to the plight of the indigenous Africans under colonisation, there is no special pleading in the text for Okonkwo. He may have been a great man, by the standards of his culture (at least the warrior standards), but he was a flawed one. He is not all that likeable, much of the time. Readers feel the pain of Obierika when he shouts out at the sight of his dead friend. They experience a sense of horror at how the DC relegates Okonkwo to the status of nothing more than an 'interesting' case study of 'pacification'. But can they entirely excuse Okonkwo for the way his own life falls apart? Like many tragic figures, his destruction was as much his own fault as that of forces beyond his control.

SAMPLE ESSAY QUESTIONS

'It is because readers feel for Okonkwo and his people that the tragedy has such force.'

Discuss.

'Okonkwo kills himself for what he thinks is a just cause, when it is really only foolish pride.'

Do you agree with this assessment?

Some people have objected that the long introductory section of *Things Fall Apart* weakens the novel. Others have a problem with the extraordinarily speedy climax, and the shock of the shift in perspective right at the end.

What is your assessment of these features of the novel?

'Okonkwo is his own worst enemy.'

Discuss.

'*Things Fall Apart* is a masterly critique of colonisation in Africa.'

Discuss.

'Those who do not bend with change will be destroyed by it. That is the overriding message of *Things Fall Apart*.'

Do you agree?

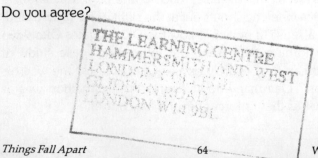
THE LEARNING CENTRE
HAMMERSMITH AND WEST
LONDON COLLEGE
GLIDDON ROAD
LONDON W14 9BL